Law and Youth Work

MARY MAGUIRE

Series Editors: Janet Batsleer and Keith Popple

LearningMatters

First published in 2009 by Learning Matters Ltd

British Library Cataloguing in Publication Data
A CIP record for this book is available from the British Library.

ISBN 978 1 84445 245 3

Cover and text design by Code 5 Design Associates Ltd
Project management by Swales & Willis
Typeset by Swales & Willis, Exeter, Devon
Printed and bound in Great Britain by TJ International Ltd, Padstow, Cornwall

Learning Matters Ltd
33 Southernhay East
Exeter EX1 1NX
Tel: 01392 215560
info@learningmatters.co.uk
www.learningmatters.co.uk

FSC
Mixed Sources
Product group from well-managed
forests and other controlled sources
Cert no. SGS-COC-2482
www.fsc.org
© 1996 Forest Stewardship Council

Law and Youth Work

Titles in the Series

To order, please contact our distributor: BEBC Distribution, Albion Close, Parkstone, Poole, BH12 3LL. Telephone: 0845 230 9000, email: **learningmatters@bebc.co.uk**. You can also find more information on each of these titles and our other learning resources at **www.learningmatters.co.uk**.

Contents

Foreword from the Series Editors

Youth work and community work has a long, rich and diverse history that spans three centuries. The development of youth work extends from the late nineteenth and early twentieth century with the emergence of voluntary groups and the serried ranks of the UK's many uniformed youth organisations, through to modern youth club work, youth project work and informal education. Youth work remains in the early twenty-first century a mixture of voluntary effort and paid and state sponsored activity.

Community work also had its beginnings in voluntary activity. Some of this activity was in the form of 'rescuing the poor', whilst community action developed as a response to oppressive circumstances and was based on the idea of self-help. In the second half of the twentieth century the state financed a good deal of local authority and government sponsored community and regeneration work and now there are multi-various community action projects and campaigns.

Today there are thousands of people involved in youth work and community work both in paid positions and in voluntary roles. However, the activity is undergoing significant change. National Occupation Standards and a new academic benchmarking statement have recently been introduced and soon all youth and community workers undertaking qualifying courses and who successfully graduate will do so with an honours degree.

Empowering Youth and Community Work Practice is a series of texts primarily aimed at students on youth and community work courses. However, more experienced practitioners from a wide range of fields will find these books useful because they offer effective ways of integrating theory, knowledge and practice. Written by experienced lecturers, practitioners and policy commentators each title covers core aspects of what is needed to be an effective practitioner and will address key competences for professional JNC recognition as a youth and community worker. The books use case studies, activities and references to the latest government initiatives to help readers learn and develop their theoretical understanding and practice. This series then will provide invaluable support to anyone studying or practising in the field of youth and community work as well as a number of other related fields.

Janet Batsleer
Manchester Metropolitan University

Keith Popple
London South Bank University

Chapter 1
Introduction

C H A P T E R   O B J E C T I V E S

The key purpose of youth work is to:

> enable young people to develop holistically, working with them to facilitate their personal, social and educational development, to enable them to develop their voice, place and influence in society and to reach their full potential.
>
> National Occupational Standards 2008

In order to meet the key purpose, the book wlll make the case for why some understanding of the law is necessary in order to help the worker to contextualise their engagement with young people. Without understanding the concept of place the worker is placed at a distinct disadvantage in empowering and enabling young people to have influence in society and develop a sense of citizenship.

This book is targeted primarily at youth workers embarking on the academic stage of their continuous professional development. It is intended to supplement your knowledge of how the developing and established law relates to your own professional practice. It does not cover all aspects of the law nor does it profess to provide all the answers to the complex issues you might face as professional workers. It should, however, help you to understand some key legal principles and provide a basis for further enquiry. It may, therefore, also be helpful to youth worker practitioners who have had limited opportunity to update themselves on developments in the law which affect their work.

It is based on fundamental principles of human rights and social justice, which lie at the heart of youth work values. The law is about values. It is also about a framework and sets of rules for regulating human behaviour. This is why it is important. A statement of youth work values taken from the National Occupational Standards for Youth Work is included, but it is worth reminding ourselves at the outset of the definition of youth work in order to determine its purpose and distinguish it from other professions that engage with young people in order to promote their social and emotional wellbeing.

Professional standards

Youth work training has undergone fairly significant changes in recent years with new qualification requirements and professional standards for practitioners. The revised Occupational Standards for Youth Work were finalised in February 2008 and cover the outcomes, behaviours, knowledge and skills that professional youth workers should conform to. Before we consider what knowledge of the law has to do with youth work, we need to understand that youth work does not operate in isolation but forms part of a range of interventions in young people's lives designed to improve their life chances. It operates within a political and social climate which has high aspirations for young people and expects high standards from those who work with them. Failures of previous policies and practices in both social and educational settings have led to a significant shift away from a less well regulated or laissez-faire approach to professional competence. There is a greater requirement to raise our professional standards if we are to create an environment where young people are able to develop and achieve higher aspirations.

Increasingly as multidisciplinary working becomes the norm, workers should expect to develop competence within their own practice areas, but to operate within a set of standards that are shared with a wider group of professional colleagues.

The occupational standards are represented in Table 1.1. You may already be familiar with them presented diagrammatically as the Summary Functional Map for Youth Work (National Occupational Standards, 2008).

Included within the table are the knowledge requirements. You will note that knowledge of legislation is explicitly listed under Section 2 which deals with the welfare and rights of young people, but it is essential in assisting you in promoting access to information and support (Section 1.4) and in understanding how youth work operates within a political and ethical environment (Section 4).

Throughout the book we will refer to key competencies to illustrate how your interpretation and application of legal principles aligns to your own professional development.

This book, therefore, considers the interrelationship between the law and professional youth work competencies. It asks you to consider which of the competencies are common to all those who engage with young people and which are those that help to distinguish youth work from other professional disciplines. It remains, therefore, quite focused on the unique perspective of the youth worker, but should help the worker to develop a better understanding of the public and professional duties of their colleagues. This, in turn, helps to equip the youth worker to provide more effective support to young people, particularly during times when intervention by other professionals becomes necessary. It may additionally help to reduce conflict between the worker and other agencies whose intervention, at least from the young person's perspective, is involuntary. It should help you to understand the rules that regulate other professions and help you to operate alongside others to get the best outcome for the young person.

There is no intention here to replace any proper legal advice or advocacy to which a young person is entitled, nor is this book a potted guide to all aspects of the law that impact on a young person. Instead it aims to combine a straightforward approach to the law as it relates to youth work with some practical exercises for the professional worker to work through independently or with colleagues.

You are encouraged to reflect on your approach to your work and consider the values that underpin your practice as well as those that underpin the development of human rights law, because it is within the framework of human rights that we will consider the impact of the law on young people. You will discover that what we value is important in

Table 1.1 National Occupational Standards – Framework

First-level function	Second-level function	Essential knowledge		
1	Facilitate the personal, social and educational development of young people	1.1	Facilitate learning and development of young people through youth work	Understanding of the impact of the broader social environment on young people's learning and development and of your own role and responsibilities as a professional worker
		1.2	plan and implement learning activities in youth work	
		1.3	promote young people's self awareness, confidence and participation	
		1.4	promote access to information and support	
2	Promote equality and young people's interests and welfare	2.1	work with young people in promoting their rights	Understanding of legislation, policy and practice which underpins a young person's human rights and basic entitlements
		2.2	safeguard the health and welfare of young people	
		2.3	promote equality and the valuing of diversity	
		2.4	fulfil regulatory and organisational requirements	

Table 1.1 (Continued)

First-level function	Second-level function	Essential knowledge		
3	Work with others	3.1	engage with young people	Understanding the perspectives and motivations of others and the impact of your own actions and behaviours
		3.2	engage with the local community	
		3.3	build working relationships and networks	
4	Develop youth work strategy and practice	4.1	establish and prioritise requirements for youth work	Understanding of the political environment and ethical framework within which youth work takes place
		4.2	plan and implement youth work strategy	
		4.3	facilitate change	
		4.4	monitor and evaluate the effectiveness of youth work strategy and plan	
5	Lead and manage teams and individuals	5.1	manage yourself	Understanding of the learning needs of others and the leadership qualities needed to create a sense of common purpose

determining how effective we become and is therefore a significant feature of your professional youth work development. Values also underpin the principles of human rights development and the development of laws affecting children and young people. This will be discussed more fully in Chapter 2, Human rights.

The core themes are set out in chapter format with an outline of what you can expect from each chapter, some exercises for you to complete and questions for you to consider. Each chapter concludes with a chapter review. There is, in addition, some suggested further reading and a list of useful websites. You are encouraged to seek out a wide range of information from different sources. Online searches can help you get started but are no substitute for reading widely to develop a good understanding of your subject through books, journals and newspapers. You should read conflicting views to enable you to critically review the literature and develop your own understanding of the impact of changes in legislation and policy in relation to young people.

In Chapter 2, the background to the development of human rights law is examined. You will be taken through different theoretical perspectives on young people's rights, from those that emphasise young people's right to self-determination to those that highlight young people's vulnerability and their right to protection and provision for their needs. You will be able to distinguish the United Nations Convention on the Rights of the Child from the European Convention on Human Rights and consider the impact of the Human Rights Act 1998 on the development of a young person's rights.

Chapter 3 looks at the legal definition of capacity and considers the extent to which young people can consent to and refuse medical treatment or interference with their bodily integrity. It examines the current position, provides the background to key judicial decisions and invites the practitioner to question the extent to which the interpretation of the law has developed insofar as it promotes young people's autonomy.

Chapter 4 is about safeguarding young people's health and wellbeing. Recent well-publicised public inquiries into child deaths have consistently highlighted the importance of effective communication between different professionals, and reinforced the notion of professional accountability, even where the professional had no direct knowledge of the facts. In this chapter we will look at some examples of cases that pose particular challenges for youth workers, and examine briefly the roles and responsibilities of other professionals. The chapter deals with the balance between confidentiality and disclosure as well as the duties and powers provided for by the Children Acts of 1989 and 2004.

In Chapter 5, there is an opportunity to take a more in-depth look at the impact of emotional distress and mental ill health on a young person's capacity to exercise their fundamental rights. It considers what protective measures the law adopts and whether there is more that could be done to intervene earlier to promote mental wellbeing.

Chapter 6 deals with crime and disorder. This is, for many youth workers, one of the most challenging to navigate as youth workers are often faced with young people who feel demonised by both the law and the wider adult communities within which they live. In this chapter we will consider current government policy and the relationship between the youth service and the youth justice agenda. We will examine the law and its relationship with the National Occupational Standards for youth workers. We will explore whether and how youth workers contribute to the development of public policy. We will ask whether there is a need to reassess youth work values in order to give effect to national policy on crime and disorder. Does the requirement in the Youth Crime Action Plan for detached youth workers and former gang members to work alongside the police to combat the 'negative effect of delinquent peer groups' equip the worker to become a more effective multi-agency worker, or does it represent a fundamental departure from core youth work values of impartiality and youth empowerment?

This leads us on to Chapter 7 in which we consider the inclusion and participation of young people in decision making and critically examine whether society's relatively recent promulgation of participation helps young people to enforce their rights or merely provides the tools for them to articulate their dissatisfaction. We look more critically at what factors the worker may need to address about their own inclusion in order to effectively promote that of young people. We will explore notions of fairness, responsibilities and arbitration.

Chapter 8 concludes with a review of the youth worker's role and takes an in-depth look at the needs of young people who face particular disadvantage because of their ethnicity, race, abilities or beliefs. It considers the young person within the context of their family and community and how the worker can ensure they meet their obligations to promote equality, value diversity and engage communities. It enables the worker to explore how they might address some of the underlying challenges and find innovative solutions to develop inclusive practice.

Who makes the law?

You are probably familiar with situations when judges appear to criticise the government, particularly when they interpret the law in ways that seem to contradict parliament's intention in creating the law in the first place. Indeed judges have not been shy in holding government ministers to account for exceeding their powers through their interpretation of the law. This is their role. Their function is to interpret the laws and apply them to the cases that come before them, but this has not stopped judges from exercising creativity in their interpretation of the law. This has sometimes led to developments in the law that were not envisaged by law makers and has led some commentators to suggest that judges play a role in making the law.

Irrespective of the power they may wield in the courtroom, laws are not made by judges but by parliament. When judges apply the law in ways that were not intended by parliament, ministers are generally fairly quick to close the loopholes that allow this to happen by creating new laws or issuing new codes of practice. In effect they find ways to curb the power of judges. This does not mean the judges remain passive in their application of the law but they must remain impartial. Judicial independence is a central principle of our constitution. It is enshrined in the European Convention on Human Rights which states: *Everyone is entitled to a fair and public hearing by an independent and impartial tribunal established by law.* (Article 6)

CASE STUDY

Article 6: Everyone is entitled to a fair and public hearing by an independent and impartial tribunal established by law.

An interesting example of how this principle applies in practice is provided by a case that came before the House of Lords, the most senior court in Britain, in 1998. The case involved the former leader of Chile, General Pinochet who, while in Britain for medical treatment was detained pending his extradition to Spain where it was intended that he be prosecuted for acts of genocide, torture and terrorism committed while he was Head of State in Chile. The disappearance of a number of Spanish citizens provided Spain with grounds for seeking his detention and extradition. General Pinochet sought release from detention by pleading immunity from prosecution. The case was heard by the House of Lords who decided by a majority of 3–2 that Pinochet should have no immunity. However, Lord Hoffman, one of the Lords deciding the case, failed to disclose his involvement with the human rights organisation Amnesty International, whose lawyers, with the leave of the court, argued successfully that the General should have no immunity.

Pinochet's lawyers then petitioned the court to lay aside the ruling and hear the case afresh on the grounds that Lord Hoffman was not impartial and should have disqualified himself from hearing the case. In a unique legal ruling a newly constituted group of law lords agreed that although justice may have been done, it was not seen to be done.

The independence of the judiciary is therefore a central theme within our constitution which, although unwritten, provides that there is a separation of powers. This means that the legislature (parliament), the executive (the government) and the judiciary (the judges) have separate and distinguishable functions. Only two roles have straddled these separate functions. One is the Lord Chancellor, who until fairly recently had an active role in government, was head of the judiciary and speaker of the House of Lords. This is no longer considered to be compatible with the notion of separation of powers.

The other person who spans all three domains is the Queen. She is the titular head of state, opening and dissolving parliament and giving assent to its laws. It is the Queen's constitutional duty to give royal assent to Acts of Parliament. She is head of the judiciary. Although not actually sitting in court, it is in her name that criminal cases are tried (*R.* v. *Brown*). The R in criminal law citations stands for *rex* or *regina* (the Latin for king or queen) depending on whether the monarch is male or female. She is also the head of the executive in that she invites newly elected prime ministers to form a government.

Figure 1.1 represents the different functions and illustrates how each separate function is under the nominal control of the crown.

How laws are made

The laws passed by parliament are called Acts of Parliament or Statutes. The body of written laws is called legislation and parliament is the legislature. When we talk about

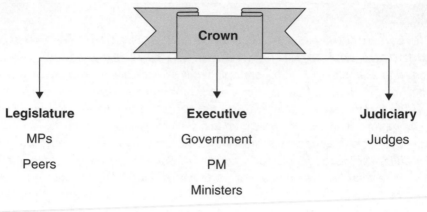

Figure 1.1 The separation of powers

statutory duties we mean those responsibilities that we have acquired as a result of legislation.

There are a number of distinct stages involved in the creation of Acts of Parliament. They provide opportunities for scrutiny by allowing debate and amendments to proposals and are an important feature of our democracy.

Most of our laws are created to resolve dilemmas or problems that arise in society and which previous laws are considered insufficient to tackle. They frequently arise from changes in government policy or through changes in government. Election manifestos are a means for politicians, if elected to form new governments, to outline their plans to make changes in the law.

The intention to make changes to the law are often announced in advance in documents such as Green or White Papers in which politicians state their intention to achieve a different result from the one that was arrived at through the application or interpretation of existing law. This might explain why we have so many criminal justice Acts. The demand for a different result is a great motivator.

ACTIVITY *1.1*

- *Give some examples of things that have resulted in changes to the law. You may be able to point to specific events which created a demand from the public or from individuals for new laws.*

- *What were the main reasons for the creation of the Children Act 2004?*

- *What was this Act of Parliament trying to remedy that was not covered by other pieces of legislation such as the Children Act 1989?*

- *Where did the demand for change come from?*

Not all laws are created when something has gone wrong in society. Some laws are created to regulate developments in medicine or technology. Many advances in technology provide particular challenges to law makers. For example, developments in and access to communications technology such as mobile phones and the internet make it difficult for governments to control and regulate many types of criminal activity, but that does not stop the public from demanding changes in the law to hold internet service providers to account.

Changes in domestic law such as the Children Act 2004 began as government policy documents. The Green Paper *Every Child Matters* heralded the government's response to the recommendations contained in the report of the public inquiry into the death of Victoria Climbié. Along with *Youth Matters* the government set out their vision for achieving better outcomes for young people and explicitly stated their intention to make changes to the law to support this objective. We will address this in detail in a later chapter but it should give you some idea of the process of law making.

The different stages of law making

Before a new law becomes an Act of Parliament it has to pass through different stages. When a law is first introduced in the House of Commons it is called a Bill. This introductory stage is called a first reading and is the way in which parliament is formally notified of the changes to the law. The Bill is published and a date set for a second reading. This allows members of parliament to prepare for the debate which takes place at the second reading and vote on whether or not they support the general principles of the Bill. This decides whether or not the Bill proceeds to the next stage. At committee stage a smaller group of MPs will undertake a more detailed examination of the Bill, take advice from experts and make any alterations or amendments.

At the third reading the amended Bill is further debated and voted on before passing to the House of Lords where it proceeds through similar stages. If there are further amendments the Bill will go back through the House of Commons for further consideration. Less controversial Bills might begin in the House of Lords.

The final stage, which happens once the Bill has passed through all these stages, is for the Queen to give Royal Assent by signing the Bill. It then becomes an Act of Parliament.

New laws do not always take immediate effect. For example, the Human Rights Act 1998 which incorporated the European Convention on Human Rights into UK law did not take effect until October 2000. This is to give those who have particular duties under the law the chance to make the necessary changes to their procedures or systems so that they are able to operate the new law. Sometimes a change in the law creates new roles for workers; often it establishes new jobs. The Race Relations (Amendment) Act, implemented as a result of the findings by the inquiry into the death of Stephen Lawrence, requires local authorities to undertake impact assessments to determine whether and to what extent their policies and practices are discriminatory. If we consider the huge number of services a local authority is responsible for providing to the public, the scale of this undertaking alone is likely to require workers to do this as part of their existing job, and therefore they will need training, or new jobs will need to be created to ensure that the Authority is not in breach of its statutory duty.

Legislation is not always implemented straight away. There may be a delay of months or even years before implementation. Laws may be implemented in full or in part with the remainder scheduled for much later. One example of this is the Family Law Act 1996 part 1 of which required divorcing couples to enter into mediation prior to divorce. The Lord Chancellor recommended the development of a national mediation service with legislation to be phased in dependent on the outcome of this scheme.

Different types of law

Most people are familiar with the difference between criminal and civil law, so this section will be fairly brief. Criminal law provides some type of sanction or punishment. When you break the law you commit a criminal offence. Ignorance of the law does not provide an excuse to break it. The age at which an individual can be charged with a crime is ten years (Crime and Disorder Act 1998). In almost all cases the state, in the name of the crown, prosecutes those who have broken the criminal law. The responsibility for proving whether or not someone has in fact committed a crime is on the prosecution. It is not for the accused to prove they are innocent but for the prosecution to prove their guilt. This is called the burden of proof. The standard of proof in criminal cases is the requirement to make the jury sure that the defendant has committed the crime. It is not enough for the jury to be persuaded that the defendant probably did it. On conviction of a crime a person acquires a criminal record.

Civil law resolves disputes between people. Proceedings are called claims. The person bringing the claim is called a claimant and the person against whom the claim is made is called the defendant. In family cases the person bringing the case is called the petitioner or applicant and the person on the other side is known as the respondent.

The Civil Procedure Rules, introduced in 1999, implemented major reforms including making the process faster, cheaper and more accessible than it had previously been. The language was modernised replacing with plain English equivalents many of the Latin phrases. If you read through older cases you are likely to come across terms such as writ (claim), plaintiff (claimant) and guardian ad litem (children's guardian).

When the case comes before the court the claimant is generally asking for some type of remedy. This could be in the form of financial compensation (damages) or might be to ask the court to instruct someone to do, or refrain from doing, something. Examples of civil law with which the professional youth worker will be more familiar include the Children Act 1989 which outlines the procedure for the local authority to follow when asking the court to make an order to protect children, and the Crime and Disorder Act 1998 which created the Antisocial Behaviour Order (ASBO). These are discussed in more detail in Chapters 4 and 6.

Figure 1.2 sets out the hierarchy of the courts and shows how they relate to each other.

You will now, hopefully, begin to understand why the law is relevant to youth work and have a better understanding of how laws are made and applied. You should be able to

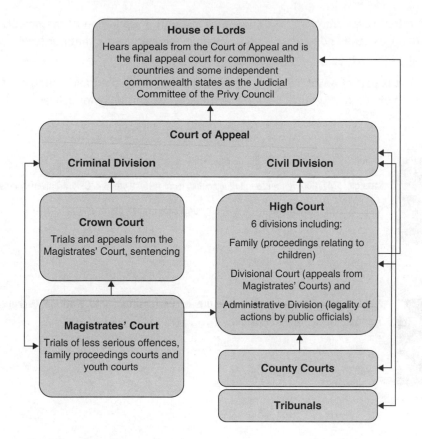

Figure 1.2 The hierarchy of the courts

distinguish between civil and criminal law. You will realise that the law will not provide rules for every situation you will encounter in the workplace; it will not help you to tackle some of the ethical issues and dilemmas within your profession, but will hopefully whet your appetite for further reading and analysis so that you can appreciate how the law regulates and supports you in your work with young people.

C H A P T E R   R E V I E W

Given the level of state intervention in young people's lives, it is important for those working with young people to have a basic understanding of how the law operates.

As integrated working becomes the model for delivering services to young people, youth workers will need to understand how the law regulates both their profession and that of their professional colleagues.

In 2008 a new set of occupational standards for youth work was published as part of the wider reform agenda. These standards are about developing a competent and effective professional workforce for young people.

The unwritten constitution in the UK operates through a separation of the powers of the legislature, executive and judiciary and it is within this framework that our legal system is developing and changing.

Youth work is part of a wider policy to deliver change for children and young people and this is given effect through the creation of legislative responsibility for delivery.

DeSmith, S and Brazier, R (1998) *Constitutional and administrative law*. Penguin.

Partington, M (2006) *Introduction to the English legal system*, 4th edn. Oxford University Press.

Rivlin, G (2006) *Understanding the law*, 4th edn. Oxford University Press.

www.lluk.org/documents/whole_suite_of_Professional_and_National_Occupational_Standards_for_Youth_Work.pdf

Children Act 1989. London: HMSO.

Family Law Act 1996. London: The Stationery Office.

Civil Procedure Rules 1998. London: The Stationery Office.

Crime and Disorder Act 1998. London: The Stationery Office.

Human Rights Act 1998. London: The Stationery Office.

Race Relations (amendment) Act 2000. London: The Stationery Office.

Every child matters Green Paper 2003. London: The Stationery Office.

Council of Europe (2002) *Convention for the protection of human rights and fundamental freedoms*. Strasbourg: Council of Europe.

Department for Education and Skills (2004) *Children Act 2004*. London: The Stationery Office.

Department for Children, Schools and Families (2008) *Youth crime action plan 2008*. London: The Stationery Office.

Lifelong Learning UK (2008) *National occupational standards for youth work*. London: Lifelong Learning UK.

United Nations (1989) *Convention on the rights of the child*. New York: Office of the United Nations High Commissioner for Human Rights.

Chapter 2
Human rights

CHAPTER OBJECTIVES

By the end of this chapter you should be able to:

- understand the impact of international treaties and European human rights law on the development of children and young people's rights in the UK;

- appreciate the distinction between the European Convention on Human Rights (ECHR) and the United Nations Convention on the Rights of the Child (UNCRC);

- consider the role the professional worker plays in the development and promotion of a culture of human rights;

- relate the role of the youth worker to the relevant occupational standards, particularly those relating to equality and young people's interests and welfare (standard 2).

Many youth workers, when asked to describe what is meant by young people's human rights, approach this question by talking about entitlements to services or by citing basic injustices young people face in their daily lives such as:

- being excluded from important decisions which affect them;

- being vilified by the press and other media;

- being accused of crime and antisocial behaviour for hanging around in groups;

- being denied access to education.

It is often easier to make assumptions about our entitlements to some of the more basic human rights, such as the right to life or the right to freedom and personal dignity. That is because, on some level, we understand that everyone is entitled to these rights and we do not therefore distinguish young people's rights from those of the general population. In this chapter we will explore in more detail some basic principles of human rights before then asking how and whether they differ in either their expression or their application to the young people with whom we work.

The idea of individual and universal human rights is not a new one. If we look at the Magna Carta signed in 1215, which limited the powers of the monarch, we can see an early recognition that those in authority do not always act in the best interests of the individual. Indeed the idea that state powers might need to be limited in the interests of its citizens has emerged over time, although with an accelerated pace during the twentieth century. This means that, although the presumption that there was a need for a written

set of common standards or laws to regulate the behaviour of the state and ensure fundamental human rights is central to the written constitutions of most modern democracies,
particular events in the last century led to the human rights development at an international level.

Before we explore this further, consider the opening paragraphs of the constitutions
of countries such as the Republic of Ireland or the United States. You will find that they
are fairly explicit about the rights that members of these states enjoy and the means
by which the powers of the state are regulated. You could argue that in both countries
there are practices that question this notion of the universality of human rights, but there
are international mechanisms for monitoring and holding countries and individuals
to account for some types of human rights violations which are outside the scope of this
book.

You might like to take some time, during the course of your studies, to find examples
of different written constitutions. Many of these can be downloaded relatively easily.
Consider the differences between them, other than the style in which they are written
and the use of language, which owes much to the fact that they were written many
years apart. What do they tell you about the rights that citizens of each of the countries
are guaranteed? You may already be familiar with some of the basic concepts. For
example, in the United States you might have heard of situations where an accused person
'takes the fifth'. This relates to the right citizens have, through the Fifth Amendment, to
avoid self-incrimination by opting not to comment or respond to questioning.

You might have noticed that you were unable to find a written constitution for the United
Kingdom. From the previous chapter you will know that this is because it operates
through a system which is known as the separation of powers, rather than having these
roles written into a formal document that everyone can read.

So do we have a right to silence as is enshrined in the US Constitution? In the United
Kingdom, the right to silence does not have the same protection it once did. Anyone who
has been cautioned (or watches UK police dramas on TV) will know that *'it may harm your
defence'* if you fail to mention something that you later wish to rely on. So what does this
now tell you about our right to rely on the first part of the caution: 'you do not have to
say anything'?

How important is it that young people are able to exercise the right not to incriminate
themselves by answering questions posed to them by the police? We might all understand
what we mean by our rights, but there could be circumstances where our ability to exercise those rights are compromised, particularly if we are told that someone is allowed to
draw negative inference from our refusal to answer questions.

You might want to undertake further reading on how the law relates to our constitution
(Rivlin, 2006) but it is not proposed to examine this in any great detail here.

Instead we will consider why young people's rights might be differentiated from rights
that are generally enjoyed by adult members of society.

In Activity 2.1 you might have included in your list the rights of children and young people
to care, shelter and protection because of their relative vulnerability, or their right to

ACTIVITY **2.1**

- *Make a list of the reasons why children and young people's rights might be considered separately from those of adult members of society.*

- *Discuss what might make it particularly challenging for people to accept the idea of young people's human rights.*

education and guidance. Did you include their right to a family life, their right to dignity and respect or their right to make decisions commensurate with their level of understanding? We will explore this later in Chapter 3 when we look at capacity and decision making in more detail.

Different authors have developed theories about children's rights. Feinberg (1980) held the view that by stating aspirational rights explicitly through international treaties, they gain credibility (if not enforceability) as rights. Freeman (1992) questions this by questioning the status of the right vested in children if its objective is to reach a societal or moral goal or aspiration which benefits others. Both Hart (1984) and Feinberg (1980) consider those who can be described as rights holders as those who are able to claim a right through the exercise of will or choice, with Hart questioning the use of the word 'rights' at all when referring to those who are too immature to claim them, such as babies and young children. MacCormick (1982), who discusses rights as interests, therefore protected by constraints on the actions of others, and O'Neill (1992) take a more protectionist line in their examination of rights as obligations on other people. They distinguish children and young people from other oppressed groups because their state of oppression is temporary.

The idea of young people's rights may be derived from internationally recognised documents such as the United Nations Convention on the Rights of the Child (UNCRC), which was formally adopted by the United Nations General Assembly in 1989. This important treaty recognises that children are rights holders and, as such, they can expect certain things in common with other children. They are not objects over which adults can exercise rights. The rights covered by the convention are extensive. They cover economic, social, cultural and political aspects of children's lives.

Within ten years of being drafted, the UNCRC had been ratified by 191 states with two notable abstentions; Somalia and the United States. The UNCRC is the first international treaty dedicated solely to the promotion and protection of children's rights and, as such, has considerable moral and political force. It is not the only international treaty that deals with human rights, but it is the first that focuses exclusively on children. You can download the full version.

However, the difficulty with the UNCRC lies in its practical application. Apart from the broad scope of its provisions, there is no mechanism for enforcement. It is not enforced through international criminal courts or through war tribunals as are other international instruments. Nor is it incorporated into domestic legislation. It has been argued (Feinberg, 1980) that it therefore remains little more than a manifesto for change. It operates as a kind of benchmark against which countries are assessed for their incorporation of human rights (Fortin, 2003).

This means that when making decisions on behalf of children and young people, while the courts may, and frequently do, take its provisions into account, they are not legally obliged to. Its provisions, although commonly cited in most policies and procedural documents on children's rights, are not enforceable.

Its persuasive potential is significant insofar as the detailed five yearly reviews undertaken can help focus attention on specific policies, such as the detention of children claiming asylum, and highlight failures to adopt the high standards of human rights expected of signatories to the Convention, but it cannot be relied on by individuals seeking redress and its embarrassment potential could be overshadowed by other more pressing and news-worthy issues.

The UN Committee on the Rights of the Child, the body established to review states' compliance with the Convention, has found in its most recent report that the UK has taken insufficient steps to implement systems to monitor and promote children's rights in the UK. This is despite radical overhaul of its children's services infrastructure in the last five years, culminating in the establishment of a Department of Children, Schools and Families, the appointment of a Minister for Children and Young People, the creation of the posts of Children's Commissioners for England, Wales, Scotland and Northern Ireland, as well as introducing significant changes in domestic legislation.

Although this might have been embarrassing for the government, the Commission's findings have had the impact of a mild rebuke rather than galvanising the government into action by addressing the infringements of children and young people's human rights that persist in the United Kingdom.

You will be familiar with the extent of media coverage in the wake of a young child's death at the hands of his or her carers. This is often coupled with a public demand for retribution against social workers and their managers for their failure to prevent such tragedies. These events naturally cause outrage and although we must not undermine the impact or horror of child murder, contrast the reporting of such incidents with the relative media silence over the daily injustice faced by a severely disabled child who is unable to access the level or type of provision that would make their life tolerable or the young person within the juvenile justice system who takes their own life. The latter is often considered to be somehow culpable and provokes us to enquire whether our demand for justice applies equally to all young people or do we apply a different standard when right to life arguments are made in respect of a severely disabled child with a life-limiting medical condition or to the young person who takes their own life in a penal institution. Do you as a professional youth worker face particular dilemmas in the course of your work when on the face of it society appears to value one human life over another?

The European Convention on Human Rights

The European Convention on Human Rights (ECHR) came into force in September 1953 in response to the human rights atrocities committed during the Second World War. The aim was to confer upon the signatories to the Convention, liability for upholding a set of basic human rights. It guaranteed citizens of signatory states a system of external scrutiny over how their rights are enforced by that state.

Unlike the United Nations Convention, the European Convention was enforceable, having an impartial court overseeing the behaviour of the countries that signed the treaty. This meant that when an individual believed that the state in which they lived operated in such a way as to severely limit their rights they could seek redress for the state's failure. This was often a cumbersome affair progressing as it did through both committee and, ultimately, the European Court for a decision, often many years after the event.

The European Convention differed from the UN Convention in a number of respects. First, it was limited to European countries, although, as we shall see later, this did not necessarily limit the impact of its decisions to European countries as it has been relied on to challenge extradition to non-European states. Second, it was not until the mid-1960s that British citizens could petition the court directly; and third, despite the fact that Britain was one of the main architects of the Convention, it was not until October 2000 that its provisions became directly enforceable in the UK through the enactment of the Human Rights Act 1998.

At the point at which the ECHR was developed, there was unlikely to be much consideration given to the separate needs and rights of young people. However, the provisions of Article 14 prevent discrimination on 'any grounds' in invoking the rights enshrined in the Convention. Theoretically at least, there is no justification for limiting access to the Convention on the grounds of age. The Convention applies, therefore, as much to children as it does to adults.

The rights are contained in a number of Convention Articles although there are various Protocols to which the UK is a party and which give citizens the right, for example, to peaceful enjoyment of possessions (First Protocol, Article 1) and education (First Protocol, Article 2).

ACTIVITY 2.2

- *Make a list of all the rights you believe are fundamental and therefore likely to be included in the ECHR. You might want to undertake this activity individually for a few minutes before discussing what is included on your list with others.*

- *Were there some rights that everyone included? Were there marked differences between the rights you started with and those you included later? Were there rights you had not considered?*

- *In small groups write a list of circumstances in which the rights might be limited. Are there some individuals, groups or situations when these rights might not apply? Are there any rights you think everyone should have irrespective of the circumstances? You might find this difficult, particularly if you feel passionately about a subject or have strong beliefs about the morality or desirability of giving everyone the same degree of protection for their human rights.*

You should have come up with a wide range of rights; those that are fundamental to our wellbeing and those that are more concerned with just processes and systems.

Let us consider for a minute what rights are included in the European Convention.

Article 1   The obligation to respect human rights

Article 2   The right to life

Article 3   Prohibition of torture

Article 4   Prohibition of slavery and forced labour

Article 5   Right to liberty and security

Article 6   Right to a fair trial

Article 7   No punishment without law

Article 8   Right to respect for private and family life

Article 9   Freedom of thought, conscience and religion

Article 10 Freedom of expression

Article 11 Freedom of assembly and association

Article 12 Right to marry

Article 13 Right to an effective remedy

Article 14 Prohibition of discrimination

There are additional provisions, within the Convention, which concern themselves with process; for example, the right to limit some of these freedoms in times of emergency, although this cannot apply to Articles 2 (except lawful acts of war), 3, 4 (paragraph 1) or 7, and the establishment of a European Court of Human Rights.

Do any of the provisions immediately strike you as having particular relevance to profes-sional youth workers? Would your answer differ if you knew that Article 3 covers inhuman and degrading treatment or punishment? We will look more closely at safeguarding young people in later chapters but Article 3 has particular relevance not only for how the state regulates young people's safety but how they are liable for failure to intervene to protect young people. This could have particular significance for the youth worker who, in attempting to build trust with a young person, is given information about a young person's exposure to harm, and treats that information in absolute confidence, thus fail-ing to act to protect the young person from further inhuman or degrading treatment.

Similarly, although Article 6 refers to a fair trial, it specifies that any hearing where deci-sions are made in respect of a young person should be conducted within a reasonable time by an independent and impartial tribunal. Do you think that our criminal or civil jus-tice systems always conform to these standards? Do youth workers have a role in helping young people to understand the obligations public bodies have towards them and ensur-ing they have a fair hearing? We will cover this in more detail in Chapter 7, but it is important to note that hearing covers a wide range of forums or panels where decisions are made about young people. If we think about neighbourhood-based panels convened to oversee antisocial behaviour (they might go by different names in different areas and include youth workers among their membership), you might want to consider whether the fact that they often exclude young people is in contravention of Article 6.

The rights protected under Article 3 have a different status to those contained within Articles 8 and 10 in that they are absolute rights and are, therefore, not subject to any qualification or restriction, nor are they derogable. This means that they apply irrespective of war or national emergency and that deviation from these rights is not justifiable on other grounds such as public health, morals or protecting the rights of others.

Many other rights protected by the ECHR are qualified in that they contain specific provisions, which specify the circumstances under which those rights can be restricted. The restrictions contained within Articles 8(2) and 10(2), for example, enable courts to take into account general public interest; such as national security, public safety, prevention of crime and disorder and, more controversially, the health, morals or rights of others. This means that the rights children have to a private and family life and to freedom of expression could be qualified by the competing rights of others.

Article 8 states that:

1 *Everyone has the right to respect for his private and family life, his home and his correspondence.*

2 *There shall be no interference by a public authority with the exercise of this right except such as in accordance with the law and is necessary in a democratic society in the interests of national security, public safety or the economic wellbeing of the country, for the prevention of disorder or crime, for the protection of health or morals, or for the protection of the rights and freedoms of others.*

The first part of Article 8 is fairly explicit. It sets out the main rights that are covered. You will notice that it covers a number of different rights: the right to a private life as well as the right to a family life; it also covers home and correspondence, that is, all the communication between you and others. Clearly it was before the days of widespread international communication via the internet but, nevertheless, this also comes within the ambit of Article 8.

In Activity 2.1 you were asked to think about situations where the rights under the Convention might be restricted. Did you include all of those above?

Before we move on to the role of the court and the application of the European Convention to the United Kingdom, did you notice that the interference with the right refers to a 'public authority'? This is important as it means that we are unable to take claims against individuals or private bodies. In order for citizens to take their grievance before the European Court, they would have to demonstrate that they had exhausted remedies within their own country and that there was something fundamentally unjust about the limitations the country (or public body) had imposed on their freedom to exercise their right.

The process is illustrated in Figure 2.1.

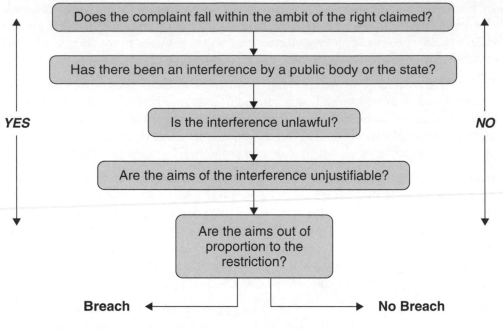

Figure 2.1 ECHR flowchart (© Hershman and McFarlane)

You will notice that cases where the UK are before the European Court are listed by the name of the parties as in *Pretty* v. *United Kingdom* (the case concerning a woman who applied to the courts for the right to live to be expanded to include the right to die), or are cited using a letter, as in *A* v. *United Kingdom*, when the identity of the applicant is protected, for example, because they are a minor. In this case A refers to a 13 year old whose stepfather had been able to use the defence of 'reasonable chastisement' available in the UK to justify cruel and inhuman treatment.

We will look at specific judgments against the UK when we examine individual rights in more detail in the relevant chapters but you should read some of the judgments yourself to get a fuller understanding of the importance the courts place on some categories of rights, such as those of press freedom and those where they are less willing to overrule national governments, for example, regarding public morals, thereby affording them a greater degree of latitude in how they interpret the rules. This is known as a margin of appreciation and you will come across it when reading about how far the courts are willing to accept that national governments should have control over issues of public morality. In *Goodwin* v. *UK*, however, the courts chose not to afford the UK a margin of appreciation in respect of the rights afforded to transsexuals, particularly in light of international trends and changing social views. Although this doctrine has been an important consideration for the European Courts, it does not apply in domestic courts as we shall see later.

One of the other doctrines developed by the European Court is that of proportionality. This refers to whether the restriction on someone's freedom is proportionate to the objective the government had in imposing the restriction in the first place. It has been argued (Hoffman and Rowe, 2006) that it plays an important part in expanding the scope of the judicial review in the United Kingdom. This is the process by which the courts are able to decide whether or not those in positions of authority have exceeded their legal powers.

The Human Rights Act 1998

The incorporation of the ECHR into UK law through the Human Rights Act (HRA) 1998, is the most significant attack on the purely welfarist approach to children's rights in evidence to date, as well as being the most significant constitutional change of our time.

The HRA was implemented on 2 October 2000 and requires the United Kingdom to give effect to the ECHR in a structured manner, the Convention becoming integrated into our law and judicial system. This has enormous significance for citizens, particularly young people, who might be aggrieved by the interpretation the courts have traditionally made of both the Children Act 1989 and the Education Act 1996. The requirement that domestic legislation is interpreted and applied consistent with the ECHR (Section 3) is a huge shift in focus away from the view that the parent is the primary consumer of both education and health care. It allows children to challenge both domestic legislation and public policy which they believe breaches the fundamental rights they enjoy under the Convention.

Courts have the power under Section 4 of the HRA to make a *declaration of incompatibility* although they are somewhat restricted in that they have no power to declare legislation unlawful. This is a marked difference of approach from that in the United States where the Supreme Court can strike out, as unlawful, the legislative provisions that are in conflict with the Bill of Rights. When a declaration of incompatibility has been made, the responsibility lies with ministers to amend primary legislation through the use of remedial orders, thus removing the incompatibility without having to invoke the full parliamentary process. This helps to speed up the process and means that the period between the breach (what went wrong) and remedy (making it right) is significantly reduced.

Although it is not part of UK law, UK courts might look to the UNCRC for guidance in interpreting the ECHR, and many judges, like those in the Strasbourg Court, will seek to apply the law to the standards intended by the UNCRC when making decisions on young people.

The effect of Section 2 of the HRA is to oblige UK courts to take European Court of Human Rights decisions into account, thereby giving the UK courts the flexibility to interpret the Act and develop UK jurisprudence on human rights. In relation to decisions on admissibility, previously taken by the European Commission (this function now lies with the Court of Human Rights following the introduction of Protocol 11), the UK courts may attach less weight to Commission decisions.

With the exception of Article 3, which prohibits torture and inhuman or degrading treatment or punishment, there is considerable scope for interpretation by each state of Articles 2–10, principally because of the qualification requirements that the rights therein can be limited if they harm the interests of others.

> ### CASE STUDY
>
> *Marcus (14) has told you that the police have sent an alcohol warning letter to his home because he was hanging about with some mates who were drinking outside the local shops.*
>
> *He says his parents 'went ballistic' and his father, after telling the police that he would sort it, 'leathered him with a belt for hanging about with louts'. He attempts to laugh it off but is upset and visibly injured. He begs you not to say anything to anyone as he does-n't want to lose face with his mates and is convinced that the police would have approved of his father's tough approach to discipline.*
>
> *In groups consider what course of action you could take? Does this present you with professional dilemmas?*

You have a number of issues to consider here. First, you might want to reassure Marcus that the degree of physical punishment he has been subjected to is excessive and therefore unlawful, and that what has happened to him is not his fault. The European Courts have determined in *A* v. *UK* that the UK were wrong to allow a stepfather who beat a young person with a stick to rely on the defence of 'reasonable chastisement', a defence allowed under the Children and Young Persons Act 1933. We will cover the recent changes in the law in more detail in the next chapter.

Second, you will need to explain that you have an obligation to act to protect Marcus and that you are unable to keep this type of incident secret, but you should reassure him that you will deal with it sensitively. Furthermore, the police are obliged, irrespective of his belief that they endorsed the punishment, to investigate and take action to protect Marcus and possibly prosecute his father. You should have protocols in place which cover the need to share this type of information with a social worker who has a duty to investigate as well as powers to act to protect Marcus. You will also want to discuss this with your own supervisor. You might want to offer some practical support to Marcus, such as accompanying him when he reports this and through any subsequent procedures, as well as being available if he wants to access further help or support.

You might already have noticed that Article 8 protects private and family life, so let us consider whether Marcus' father can rely on this to protect his right to invoke privacy and family life in order to impose discipline without interference from public authorities such as social workers or police.

You will see from the way in which this provision is worded, the exercise of this right is limited to 'operating within the law' and ensuring the protection of the health, rights and freedoms of others.

Although Article 3 rights are not qualified, they are unique in this respect insofar as the freedoms protected under other Articles of the European Convention are restricted if they interfere with a well-functioning, democratic and free society and the freedoms, health and morals of other people. It has been argued that physical punishment of children and young people is never justifiable as the prevention of inhuman and degrading treatment and punishment are not qualified and therefore do not need to be balanced against any alternative justification. You might want to look at the consultation document *Protecting children, supporting parents* (Department of Health, 1995) and the press coverage of the ensuing heated debates at the time on parents' rights to discipline children and the extent to which they could do this provided they avoided injury to the child's brain, ears or eyes. Do you have a view on how far the professional worker should interfere with parents' behaviour in disciplining their children? Does your personal view conflict with your professional duties?

Human rights laws do not cover all the aspects of Marcus' situation. Many of the issues you face in a situation such as that presented within the case study are dependent on your professionalism as a worker. They concern your relationship with others and how you develop this in order to secure the best outcome for the young person or people with whom you are working.

Rarely is the worker confronted with a clear-cut case where there is a straightforward course of action; support, report and record. You will need to refer back to the previous chapter to look at which National Occupational Standards are relevant to the different situations within which you find yourself. You might have noticed the relevance to a number of different standards on empowering young people and enabling them to take measures to protect themselves.

The role of the youth worker

Let us consider some of the wider issues involved in this particular case as they apply to how effectively the youth worker operates with other professional colleagues in finding the right balance between supporting and enabling the young person to develop as an autonomous human being able to make their own decisions and learning to take risks that do not harm others, and being part of a society where increasing exposure to harmful risks causes real problems for the young person and for their wider community.

Take for example the increasing emphasis on addressing young people's alcohol use. The professional youth worker is likely to be working alongside a wide range of organisations or professionals towards a set of common objectives such as: reducing alcohol use in public, prohibiting alcohol sales to minors and offering treatment to those young people who become dependent on alcohol. Yet the professional youth worker may find that their role in multidisciplinary work is confined to providing diversionary activities which create alternatives for young people drinking in public, whereas they would rather be valued for their contribution to addressing underlying causes.

It is likely that the youth worker will take a different professional view to that of other agencies involved. For example, the local authority's environmental protection officer's main role is to identify and prosecute those who supply alcohol to minors. They might involve young people in 'test purchasing' in order to help identify those who are breaking the law, but they are unlikely to have much involvement with the young people themselves.

The police role is to prevent the commission of crime both by the supplier and the person drinking on the streets. Drug and alcohol services are more likely to look at the health impacts and offer a range of services including advice and access to treatment for young people who use or become dependent on alcohol or other substances. They might offer support to other family members. Social workers are likely to be concerned primarily with the need to protect young people and ensure that those responsible for their care are not neglecting their duties.

You will, hopefully, already begin to see how the youth work role can be developed in this context, so that it extends beyond the responsibility for diverting young people from crime and antisocial behaviour with some well-designed alternative provision.

We will undertake an examination of the youth work role in more detail in different contexts in later chapters of this book, but you should hopefully begin to see how human rights law seeks to find a balance between the rights that can be enjoyed by young people and the limitations on those rights when they interfere with the rights of others. This is a recurrent theme within this book.

You might want to think about what particular skills the youth worker can employ and how these relate to the National Occupational Standards (see Table 1.1). Good interpersonal, effective negotiation and conflict resolution skills are essential in enabling the worker to be a team worker. Hearing the different perspectives that other agencies and individuals bring to multidisciplinary work around wider social issues is an occupational requirement (Section 3). Can you use these skills to best effect when promoting and championing young people's rights? They can also help you in developing and delivering the youth work strategy (Section 4.2) and facilitating change (Section 4.3).

And, finally, a note on the non-incorporation of Article 13. Article 13, which provides complainants with an effective remedy before a national authority, has not been incorporated into UK law. Remedies can now be secured under Sections 6 and 7 of the HRA.

Section 6 provides that:

> *it is unlawful for a Public Authority to act* [including failure to act – Section 6(6)] *in a way which is incompatible with a convention right*.

And Section 7 provides the remedy for failure of the local authority to act consistently with their obligations under Section 6(1).

The effects of Sections 6 and 7 are to give children some latitude in challenging decisions made by the local authority. Local Authorities across the United Kingdom will undoubtedly continue to be compelled to scrutinise all their procedures to ensure that decisions they make in respect of children have a sound foundation, or face numerous challenges under the HRA over compliance with the Convention.

In UK law, courts have been able in the past to determine that there are some circumstances when civil action taken against a public authority ought to be disallowed on public policy grounds, the argument being that the cost of allowing such an action would interfere with the proper running of the public body. This was considered, as was the issue of immunity from liability in negligence, in *Z and TP and KM (T.P. and*

K.M. v. *United Kingdom, Strasbourg (Application no. 28945/95) 10 May 2001)*. These public policy arguments accepted by the UK courts were lodged with the Commission alleging violation of a number of rights, including the right to an effective remedy under domestic law.

Finding for the applicants under Article 13, the judgment did not accept the House of Lords decision, finding instead that the reluctance to extend the local authority's duty of care to the applicants amounted to immunity from suit for the local authority and there-fore a breach of Article 6. This meant that the decision of the highest court in the land was questioned about its allowing the government to avoid their duties under the law.

Remedies for negligent acts or omissions, on the part of the public agencies acting under statutory duty, are now secured under Section 7 of the HRA. The non-retrospective nature of the provision means that some people could still be denied an effective remedy and that some cases of this nature will inevitably come before the courts in Strasbourg.

In interpreting the Convention the courts have at their disposal the judgments of the European Court and the decisions (on admissibility) of the European Commission. The weight they will give to the latter is debatable but the judgments provide guidance to the UK courts in applying the HRA consistently.

The approach taken by the Strasbourg Court to interpreting the Convention, as well as the substantial body of European case law, provides the UK courts with guidance on how the Convention must be complied with. It might also help you to assess whether the restriction to the freedom is proportionate, and marshal your arguments for achieving a fairer balance when you are advocating on behalf of young people in your professional work.

Although it proposed to examine the rights arising in respect of children under each of the key Articles separately, there will be some overlap as individuals experience violation of a number of Convention rights. For example, a case involving removal of children into public care or transferring them into psychiatric care in order to treat them could invoke rights under both Articles 3 and 8.

It is also worth noting that discrimination (Article 14) refers to discrimination in how the rights are invoked or on how the limitations apply. There is no separate right to challenge under this provision. This means that Article 14 can only be cited if it relates to violations under other provisions of the European Convention.

Compatibility with the Convention

There is a duty on parliament to create new legislation that is compatible with the rights under the European Convention and to amend legislation that is incompatible. The courts in the UK will make a declaration of incompatibility where it arises and it is then the responsibility of parliament to amend the law to remove the incompatibility. Where there is some ambiguity, the courts will interpret the legislation according to the spirit of the Convention rights, often taking into consideration the United Nations Convention, despite its non-enforceable status.

C H A P T E R   R E V I E W

- The UNCRC is the first international treaty to focus directly on children.

- The ECHR, developed in the aftermath of the Second World War, created an enforceable set of human rights on which citizens of states which signed up could rely.

- ECHR cases are heard by the Court of Human Rights in Strasbourg.

- The ECHR is directly enforceable in the United Kingdom since the HRA (1998) became law in October 2000.

- Children and young people have equality before the law and the law will seek to find the right balance between conflicting human rights.

FURTHER READING

Harvey, C (ed) (2005) *Human rights in the community: rights as agents for change.* Oxford: Hart.

Hoffman, D and Rowe, J (2006) *Human rights in the UK: an introduction to the Human Rights Act 1998.* Harlow, Essex: Pearson Education.

Rivlin, G (2006) *Understanding the law.* Oxford: OUP.

Willow, C (2005) Children's human rights as a force for change, in Harvey, C (ed) *Human rights in the community: rights as agents for change.* Oxford: Hart.

WEBSITES

http://193.178.1.117/attached_files/Pdf%20files/Constitution%20of%20IrelandNov2004.pdf

www.crin.org/docs/resources/treaties/uncrc.psp

www.echr.coe.int/echr

www.direct.gov.uk

www.unicef.org.uk/youthvoice

www.usconstitution.net/const.html

REFERENCES

Children and Young Persons Act 1933. London: HMSO.

Children Act 1989. London: HMSO.

Education Act 1996. London: The Stationery Office.

Human Rights Act 1998. London: The Stationery Office.

Council of Europe (2002) *Convention for the protection of human rights and fundamental freedoms.* Strasbourg: Council of Europe.

Feinberg, J (1980) *Rights, justice and the bounds of liberty.* Princeton University Press.

Fortin, J (2003) *Children's rights and the developing law.* London: LexisNexis.

Freeman, M (1992) The limits of children's rights, in Freeman, M and Veerman, P (eds) *The ideologies of children's rights.* Dordrecht: Martinus Nijhoff.

Hart, HLA (1984) Are there any natural rights?, in Waldron, J (ed) *Theories of rights.* Oxford: OUP.

Department of Health (2000) *Protecting children, supporting parents.* London: DoH.

Hoffman, D and Rowe, J (2006) *Human rights in the UK: an introduction to the Human Rights Act 1998.* Harlow, Essex: Pearson Education.

Howard, AED (1988) *Magna Carta: text and commentary.* Charlottesville: University of Virginia.

Lifelong Learning UK (2008) *National occupational standards for youth work.* London: Lifelong Learning UK.

MacCormick, N (1982) *Legal right and social democracy: essays on legal and political philosophy.* Oxford: Clarendon Press.

O'Neill, O (1992) Children's rights and children's lives, in Alson, P, Parker, S and Seymour, J (eds) *Children's rights and the law.* Oxford: Clarendon Press.

Rivlin, G (2006) *Understanding the law.* Oxford: Oxford University Press.

United Nations (1989) *Convention on the rights of the child.* New York: Office of the United Nations High Commissioner for Human Rights.

Chapter 3
Autonomy, consent and competence

```
                    C H A P T E R   O B J E C T I V E S
```

By the end of this chapter the youth worker should:

- have a more comprehensive understanding of why consent is important from an ethical or moral perspective; and

- understand why it is essential from a legal perspective.

In addition this chapter:

- supplements the knowledge you have acquired about young people's growing capacity and emergence into adulthood and looks at the application of that theory and its impact on young people's lives;

- examines what factors have been taken into account by policy makers and judges when deciding whether young people's ability to consent (competence) is based on their age, emotional maturity or on wider social considerations;

- enables the youth worker to reflect on situations they might face or have already faced within their own professional practice where they experience conflict over whose rights prevail; the young person's, the parent's or the professional's;

- offers some examples of the risks to young people's health and wellbeing for the worker to consider when advising or supporting a young person who is making choices without fully understanding the consequences of their actions;

- encourages you to undertake further enquiry and to develop your own analytical skills; hearing what rationale judges have employed when reaching sometimes radical and often contentious decisions which have wide-ranging implications for young people;

- will hopefully make you a better informed, thoughtful practitioner.

In the previous chapter we looked at human rights and explored the importance of respect for the individual's autonomy or right to self-determination. You were also invited to consider the distinction between legal and ethical rights; those that are enforceable and those that are morally just but for which there is no legal protection. This chapter is concerned with consent and examines what valid consent means and why this is so important when working with young people.

If we start with the assumption that everyone is entitled to bodily integrity and that to interfere with that right without good cause is not just unethical but may also be unlawful, we can begin to understand why consent is so important.

Consent is the ethical and legal expression of our fundamental human right to bodily integrity and self-determination. Without consent any physical contact with another person, whether this is intentional or negligent, could potentially be regarded as battery. This might seem extreme if we consider the types of physical contact that would be regarded as normal or routine or, indeed, the number of sports and other physical activities where it is expected.

It is fair to say that consent to certain activities is implied as people willingly take part in contact sports. The rules that govern these types of activities cover what is and what is not allowed. For example, it is generally accepted that in football it is the ball that is kicked, not your opponent. Similarly, emergency medical treatment given to an unconscious accident victim would not normally interfere with an individual's right to respect for their bodily integrity, although, as we shall see later, lifesaving treatment that is refused by a competent person can be considered an unlawful interference with an individual's right.

Along with assault and false imprisonment, battery is one of the types of activities that interfere with someone's bodily integrity. It can be dealt with through both civil and criminal actions.

Most professional youth workers would broadly accept that obtaining consent from someone is not only necessary in order to provide protection from civil proceedings or criminal prosecution, but is the respectful thing to do when interacting with others. It is part of the youth worker's training to apply this principle equally to all young people they come into contact with in the course of their work. However, there is still some uncertainty among workers about whom consent should be obtained from and in what circumstances it is advisable to obtain parental consent rather than rely on the young person's ability to make a decision to undertake particular activities.

In the previous chapter we looked at the rights of young people to protection as well as their right to emerge into adulthood equipped with the skills to make decisions in their own right.

The fact that they work primarily with young people in transition from childhood to adulthood means that youth workers will regularly have to consider how they balance the obligation to respect a young person's growing autonomy throughout adolescence, thus equipping them with the skills to make this transition successfully, and ensuring that the young person themselves has the full benefit of protection from harm.

The professional youth worker needs to be mindful of the fact that the law provides a greater degree of protection for young people than it does for adults, not just to prevent others from harming them but to prevent a young person from making a decision that has the potential for causing future harm. The young person's right to self-determination might sometimes conflict with their right to be protected, and this may pose a dilemma for the youth worker. It is important for the worker to operate within the guidelines set out in law and by their employer, seeking guidance if necessary from their supervisor when they are unclear about the correct course of action to take.

Youth workers will already be familiar with the principle of obtaining consent for young people to take part in certain types of activities, generally those that are considered to carry some risk and require a degree of supervision.

Make a list of activities for which a youth worker is likely to require consent before undertaking.

Then make a second list of who you think is able to provide consent. We will review this at the end of the chapter.

Do the activities on your list require explicit consent from the young person themselves, or do the majority of activities require parental consent? Have you considered situations when the young person does not live with their parent?

Did your list include activities such as providing advice on contraception, abortion or harm minimisation (e.g. safer sex, safer drug use)?

Although the principles of obtaining consent have much wider application, it is in the provision of advice on health and wellbeing that workers need to be very clear about what they are permitted to do.

The worker needs to operate to consistently high professional standards and have a good understanding of their legal obligations towards young people. This is why it is so important to seek support and advice from your supervisor when dealing with issues that concern young people's health and wellbeing, and to ensure that you have access to relevant guidance if needed. Most youth workers will be working within large organisations, either statutory such as local authorities, or voluntary, which will have published guidance as well as access to legal advice for workers who are working with vulnerable young people and are uncertain about their position.

Capacity to consent

Let us consider what the law says about whether a young person can consent for themselves. Until relatively recently, it was widely understood that until the young person reached a specified age, only a parent could give valid consent. This was based, in part, on a presumption that parents always act in the best interests of their child and that no conflict existed between parents' wishes and those of their offspring. This was undoubtedly the presumption made by Victoria Gillick in a landmark case that has established the rules on obtaining consent from young people.

The case, which was eventually decided in the House of Lords, made medical history and forms the basis for what is now known as the Fraser guidelines (named after one of the judges in the case who defined the criteria for deciding whether a young person is competent to give consent).

The background to the decision in *Gillick v. West Norfolk and Wisbech Area Health Authority* is that Victoria Gillick, a mother of daughters who were under 16, challenged a circular issued to doctors by the government allowing them to give contraceptive advice to young people under the age of 16 without obtaining prior consent from their parents.

The main considerations in Gillick were as follows. First, the courts considered the ambit of Section 8 of the *Family Law Reform Act 1969* which recognised that a 16 year old could consent to medical treatment in their own right. Gillick argued that, therefore, the presumption was that parental consent was required for those who are under 16 and that doctors had a duty to seek parental consent.

Second, it was argued that as the age of consent to sexual intercourse was 16, doctors providing contraceptive advice to a child under 16 were aiding and abetting an unlawful act which was there to protect children from sexual exploitation, and that they should not have protection from prosecution.

The case itself makes interesting reading as it gives some indication of the variation in opinion among the judges who heard it. You might want to check this out for yourself as it is widely reported in a number of medical law textbooks. Gillick's argument was accepted by the majority of judges who heard it overall, but because it was decided in the House of Lords, the most senior court, by a three to two majority, the most senior judges disagreed with Gillick, deciding instead that there could be no fixed age at which a young person became competent and that it would go against the notion that young people's competence to make decisions increases as they get older. This rather liberal approach accepted that the nature of growing up and approaching adulthood conferred on the young person a greater degree of control over their own body.

It has been argued that the greater social need of reducing risk of early pregnancy for sexually active young people might have played some part in the reasoning, but at the time it was considered to be a watershed in self-determination for the young person. Lord Scarman, who was one of the deciding judges, considered that parental rights to consent ended when the young person reached the point when he or she: . . . *achieves a sufficient understanding and intelligence to enable him or her to understand fully what is proposed.*

Lord Fraser expressed the view that parental rights were there to benefit the child not the parent and were, therefore, exercisable only insofar as they enabled the parent to fulfil their duties towards their children. He set out the criteria that could be used by doctors to assess whether a young person was sufficiently competent to give the required consent. It will be familiar to many of you in your work with young women seeking contraceptive advice.

1 the girl understands the advice;

2 the doctor cannot persuade her to inform her parents or allow them to be informed;

3 she is likely to have sex with or without the advice;

4 her physical or mental health would suffer without the advice;

5 her best interests require the advice/treatment to be given without parental consent.

These principles were subsequently incorporated into Department of Health guidance although they have practical application in other circumstances and are widely applied.

Since Gillick there have been a number of challenges in the courts, mainly on the rights of parents to demand treatment in the face of medical opinion to the contrary, and generally concerning younger children with disabilities. This has meant that the debate on parental rights and obligations has been a recurrent theme over the years, although it is clear from these cases that it is the recommendations of medical professionals that prevail.

In 2006 the High Court was asked to review the position on whether a young person was entitled to the privacy established by Gillick when they sought contraceptive advice and abortion. In reissuing the Best Practice Guidance, another parent, Sue Axon, claimed that the guidance misrepresented the effect of Gillick and excluded parents from offering the right level of support to their child in the event that they sought an abortion. She also argued that to afford the young person complete confidentiality interfered with the parents' human rights to a 'private and family life'.

The High Court disagreed, holding that the position established by Gillick remained unchanged and that the parents' rights to a family life gave way to an adolescent's right to confidentiality. The Court was keen to reinforce the principle of confidentiality particularly given the significant evidence from research that a failure to guarantee confidentiality would most likely result in a huge reduction in the numbers of young people seeking advice on contraception and sexually transmitted diseases, with far-reaching consequences.

Competence to refuse treatment

You have seen how the law operates to acknowledge a young person's growing autonomy and right to consent to treatment that promotes their health and wellbeing. We will now consider whether the right to consent to medical treatment extends to the right to refuse medical treatment.

ACTIVITY **3.2**

Consider the following example from professional practice.

You are working with a 14-year-old young man who is anorexic and has visible injuries as a result of harming himself. You have spoken to him about this, but he tells you it is his body and he has a right to do what he wants with it.

Do you think he is right? You might want to discuss this with colleagues. Take about 20 minutes.

What reasons might be given for limiting young people's right to refuse treatment?

It is generally accepted that a competent adult can refuse medical treatment even if that decision results in their death. The most well-known examples of this are where adults refuse, for religious reasons, to accept blood transfusions or transplants.

The law supports this right and will rarely deviate from this to override this right to self-determination by a competent adult. It is a matter for the courts to determine whether the adult is competent, and this has been the subject of a number of rulings, for example, in the case of notorious murderer Ian Brady who went on hunger strike in an effort to end his life. In that case the court decided he was not competent to make the decision and ordered that he be treated against his will.

The law is much more reticent to afford the same level of autonomous decision making to young people who refuse treatment.

The first case following Gillick which came before the courts and tested this was that of a 15-year-old girl *Re R (1992)* who was placed, by the local authority, in an adolescent psychiatric unit, following a period of disturbed behaviour where she had experienced hallucinations and had threatened suicide.

During periods when she was lucid and when it *was* accepted, by the local authority, that she understood the nature and effect of the medication prescribed, she refused to take it. Initially the local authority complied with her wishes but under pressure from the unit, which was no longer prepared to care for her, it commenced wardship proceedings and sought the court's permission to administer anti-psychotic drugs with or without her consent.

The court had to consider whether R was Gillick-competent and if not who could give consent on her behalf. Lord Donaldson MR confirmed that consent to treat did not create an obligation on medical staff to provide treatment but merely allowed them to treat when someone provided the required consent. He likened the provision of consent to that of being a keyholder; namely, that consent merely unlocked the door (to medical treatment) and could therefore be provided by anyone who held the key. Because R was a ward of the court, the court was now the keyholder and therefore able to consent on behalf of the young woman.

The following year another case came before the courts. This time the courts were faced with a refusal of treatment by an anorexic 16 year old. W was a young woman who was admitted to an adolescent residential unit. She was objecting to a proposed move to a hospital specialising in the treatment of eating disorders.

This case, like Gillick, concerned the interpretation of Section 8 of the Family Law Reform Act 1969. Section 8(1) provides that:

> *The consent of a minor who has attained the age of sixteen years to any surgical,*
> *medical or dental treatment which, in the absence of consent would constitute*
> *a trespass to his person, shall be effective as it would be if he were of full age; and*
> *where a minor has by virtue of this section given an effective consent for an*
> *effective treatment it shall not be necessary to obtain any consent for it from his*
> *parent or guardian.*

While the argument in Gillick centred on whether Section 8 created an assumption that consent was needed to treat young people under 16, the court in W was now concerned with whether Section 8 allowed a 16 year old to refuse treatment as though she were over 18.

In order to interpret the law, the court had to consider what was intended by parliament when they enacted the law. The Act followed a report by the Lacey Committee in the late 1960s, which considered the age of majority. The committee reported on the untenable position that faced the many 16–21 year olds who lived away from home but were sub-jected to unnecessary suffering by being unable to access urgent but non-emergency treatment because the treatment they needed required parental consent. The committee were also concerned at the refusal of young women, for whom therapeutic abortion was recommended, to attend hospital unless their privacy was guaranteed.

In both these circumstances doctors were prohibited from offering the required treatment.

The committee also considered whether a refusal of treatment should be effective but did not recommend its inclusion, nor did parliament make provision for it in Section 8.

Furthermore, Lord Donaldson MR distinguished the two underlying purposes of obtaining consent:

- *clinical*: a compliant patient has confidence in the treatment and is more likely to benefit from it; and
- *legal*: the doctor is protected from criminal charge of battery or a civil claim for damages.

He stated that the main purpose of Section 8 was to protect the doctor and that he regretted his earlier keyholder analogy, preferring instead to see consent as a flak jacket that protected the medic from litigious patients.

Ultimately, the decision in R was that the nature of the disease, anorexia nervosa, had caused the young woman to fail to recognise the irreversible consequences of her actions and that she was unaware of how ill she had become during the course of the hearing.

He recognised that R had not refused all treatment but the selective nature of what she was consenting to was a feature of the controlling influence of anorexia. This inability to reason rendered her incapable of making an informed choice. It was therefore the respon-sibility of the court to intervene under its own inherent jurisdiction and provide the necessary consent to remove her to the specialist hospital for treatment in the face of R's objection.

ACTIVITY 3.3

- *Do you agree with the court's reasoning?*
- *What other reasons might the courts have for intervening when young people refuse treatment?*
- *Compare the reasons offered by different judges in these cases and some of the com-mentary offered by writers on the subject.*

Although these decisions concern medical treatment, it should come as no surprise that it is within the ambit of health care and decision making that the important principle of bodily integrity is defined. It is important for the youth worker to examine the extent to which these decisions inform policy and practice in work with young people.

The right to control over our bodies is a fundamental human right and, whether we view consent as a key or a flak jacket, its importance as the valid expression of an individual's human right to respect for their body is not one to be taken lightly.

The youth worker is likely to come across a wide range of situations where the issue of consent is relevant other than those that involve health care, but the principles of self-determination and decision making are the same. In addition, many youth workers will operate within multidisciplinary teams, where colleagues from other professional backgrounds are likely to hold different views on issues of confidentiality, consent and young people's rights to self-determination. Hopefully you now feel better equipped to understand consent in the context of a young person's human rights and confident about your ability to represent the current state of the law.

In Activity 3.1 you were asked to list the people who could give consent on behalf of the young person. Did you include the courts? You should also have included anyone who has parental responsibility for the young person as well as what you have learned about situations where the young person can consent on their own behalf.

Although there is no set lower age at which a young person becomes competent, most professionals take the precaution of obtaining valid consent from the person with parental responsibility before engaging young people in activities that carry a high risk. This does not excuse professionals who act negligently, but helps inform everyone of the nature and likelihood of the risk involved. Although there is no doctrine of informed consent within the UK, professionals working with young people are generally required to undertake risk assessments as part of their work and in any case this is good practice.

Did you know?

Not all of the people with whom the young person lives or, indeed, all of those who routinely sign consent forms on their behalf, are able to provide valid consent. You are likely to come across situations where the young person has obtained consent from someone who is not entitled to give it. The points for reflection below give a summary of the people who have parental responsibility. You might find it useful as a professional and within your personal lives to consider the nature of that responsibility, which is defined in the Children Act 1989 as: *all the rights, duties, powers, responsibilities and authority which by law a parent of a child has in relation to the child and his property*.

This may include:

- making choices about a child or young person's religion, education, name and where they will live;
- making decisions about medical treatment (including blood tests);
- discipline;
- leaving the country, perhaps for a holiday;
- representing the child in legal proceedings.

Points for reflection

People with parental responsibility

The following people have parental responsibility:

- the mother of a child (this can only be removed if a child is adopted or placed for adoption);
- the married father of a child;
- the unmarried father, **only if**:
  - *the birth was registered before 1 December 2003* **and** the mother has signed a parental responsibility agreement, **or** the court has made a parental responsibility order;
  - *the birth was registered after 1 December 2003* **and** he is named as the father on the birth certificate;
- a step-parent, provided that all those with parental responsibility agree in writing;
- a civil partner with the agreement of the other partner if they have PR (if both parents have PR, agreement is needed from each);
- anyone who has a residence order as long as the order is in force;
- the local authority if a care order has been made;
- adoptive parents;
- someone appointed as the child's legal guardian;
- the holder of a Special Guardianship Order.

(www.askthefamilylawyer.co.uk)

C H A P T E R R E V I E W

- Without consent, unlawful physical contact may give rise to a criminal charge of battery or a civil action for damages for trespass to the person.
- There is no fixed age at which a child/young person becomes competent to consent.
- A leading case on a young person's competence to consent is *Gillick* v. *West Norfolk and Wisbech Area Health Authority*.
- Fraser guidelines (named after one of the judges in *Gillick*) set the criteria by which competence is assessed.
- There is no absolute right to refuse treatment if under 18 years of age, (re R and re W) and the court's permission must be sought when a competent minor refuses treatment which the medical practitioner considers essential.

- If a child/young person is not competent, a person with parental responsibility can give consent on their behalf.

- Young people who are deemed competent are entitled to privacy.

- The Children Act 1989 defined the nature of parental responsibility.

- Everyone (including the young person) is entitled to respect for their private and family life (Human Rights Act 1998).

FURTHER READING

Baxter, C, Brennan, MG, Coldicott, Y and Möller, M (2005) *The practical guide to medical ethics and law*, 2nd edn. Cheshire: PasTest Ltd.

Mason, JK and McCall Smith, RA (1999) *Law and medical ethics*, 5th edn. London: Butterworth-Heinemann.

McHale, J and Fox, M (with Murphy, J) (1999) *Health care law*. London: Sweet and Maxwell.

REFERENCES

Children Act 1989. London: HMSO.

Family Law Reform Act 1969. London: HMSO.

Sexual Offences Act 1956. London: HMSO.

Department of Health (2004) *Best practice guidance for doctors and other health professionals on the provision of advice and treatment to young people under 16 on contraception, sexual and reproductive health.* London: DoH.

Fraser, Lord (1985) *Fraser guidelines on obtaining consent.* www.surreycc.gov.uk/sccwebsite/sccws-pages.nsf/LookupWebPagesByTITLE_RTF/The+Fraser+Guidelines?opendocumen

Hall, A (2006) Children's rights, parents' wishes and the state: the medical treatment of children. *Family Law*, 36: 317–22.

Report of the Committee on the Age of Majority 1967 (Cmnd 3342). London: Hansard.

CASES

Gillick v. *West Norfolk Health Authority* [1986] AC 112, [1985] All ER 533.

The Queen on the Application of Sue Axon v. *The Secretary of State for Health* (The Family Planning Association: intervening) [2006] EWCA 37 (Admin).

Re R (A Minor) (Wardship; Medical Treatment) [1991] 4 All E.R. 177, [1922] Fam 11, [1991] 3 W.L.R. 592.

Chapter 4
Child protection

In her book *Children's rights and the developing law*, Jane Fortin poses the following dilemma:

> *the degree of state surveillance and control necessary to prevent all ill-treatment would involve an unacceptable interference with the upbringing of many thousands of children, the majority of whom are perfectly well cared for by loving parents.*

(page 447)

Do you agree with this statement? It is a sad fact that although many young people suffer from preventable harm, there are a significant number who do not get the help they need because their age, language or communication skills, emotional and mental health needs or their lack of access to services makes them particularly vulnerable. Many young people at risk have learned, either because of threats or shame, to hide their ill-treatment from those professionals who might be able to help.

Yet after each enquiry into the death of a child examining what went wrong, who acted ineffectively or who failed to act when they should have acted, the burden on professionals working with children and young people to demonstrate whether they have undertaken a sufficient level of surveillance increases.

Nor are the demands on the professional worker confined to tragic incidents where children are killed or seriously injured. Those working with young people face ever-increasing demands to intervene effectively to prevent youth crime or antisocial behaviour, reduce the rate of teenage pregnancy and protect young people from sexual exploitation. In short, the expectations we have of workers to exert sufficient influence and control over young people in order to prevent a wide range of social ills is very high.

Do you think youth workers have struck the right balance between engaging with and building trust among young people and taking action which could have the effect of damaging trust but ultimately prevents a greater harm?

In this chapter we will examine more closely the requirement to protect young people from harm. Although we are concerned primarily with the role of the youth worker, this can be best understood when we look at the wider developments in child protection policy and law over the last 30 years and discover why it is no longer acceptable to think of safeguarding as someone else's job.

At the end of the chapter we will consider the scope and potential impact of a relatively new duty (under the Children Act 2004) to cooperate with others to promote wellbeing. This duty is much wider in scope than that required under previous legislation (Children Act 1989) where a 'risk of significant harm' had to be met before the legal duty to investigate or intervene could be fully justified.

It is inevitable that, within your professional practice, you will have to make a judgement about when to take specific action to protect a young person you come into contact with.

ACTIVITY 4.1

Can you give reasons why the youth worker may refrain from acting when they suspect or are told that a young person is at risk?

You might have included some of the following in your answer to Activity 4.1.

- The worker has been told by the young person that social workers and/or police are already involved.

- There is insufficient information given by the young person to enable the worker to know how great the level of risk is and who is at risk.

- A worker is concerned that they could be breaching a young person's trust as the information is given in confidence and that if they take action the young person will deny it.

- The worker lacks confidence in their own judgement, knowledge or skills.

- The worker's experience of having taken action in the past has been a negative one.

These reasons have been cited by professionals as some of the dilemmas they face in determining who to notify and at what point. Many workers who have experience of supporting young people through an investigative stage or through subsequent court proceedings lack faith in the systems themselves and this can also act as a barrier to their taking responsibility for reporting and acting on information they are given by young people.

Points for reflection

Did you know that your duties to safeguard young people not only require you to act but could make you liable for your failure to act (*Z and others* v. *United Kingdom*)?

In the previous chapter we looked at the emerging independence of young people and considered the tensions between empowering and enabling young people to take responsibility for their own lives and offering them the right level of support and advice without undermining them or disregarding the decisions they make.

It is, therefore, easier to establish a duty to protect children and young people when they are young, relatively immature, have a physical disability, learning difficulty or mental health need. Similarly, when we become aware that a young person is being physically or sexually abused in the home or by a trusted adult it is obvious to most workers what course of action must be taken.

The real challenge lies in knowing when and how to intervene when the circumstances are less clear cut. Taking risks is, however, a normal part of adolescence and it is more difficult to establish a clear line between a young person's autonomy over their body, their capacity and right to make decisions for themselves and the degree of risk they are exposed to.

ACTIVITY 4.2

Consider the following situations and decide which of the following three courses of action you would take.

a Do nothing, this is a low risk.

b Make a referral to another agency or professional and check progress with them.

c Take immediate protective action and notify police and/or social work child protection services.

You can either complete this activity individually or within a group. If working with colleagues, make a record of the agreed action and note reasons for disagreement. You will note that 'get a fuller picture' or 'investigate further' are not included in the options, so try to make a decision on the information provided.

1. A 12-year-old girl is hanging around the centre at night because there is no one at home.

2. A 14 year old is the main carer for a parent with significant mental health problems.

3. A teenage parent regularly leaves a baby in the care of a 14 year old you are working with.

4. A 15-year-old young woman has told you she is fearful of going on a planned holiday to Pakistan as she has overheard that she is to be married to her mum's cousin.

5. A 14-year-old girl is planning to meet with her internet boyfriend.

Did you find Activity 4.2 difficult? In discussing this with other youth workers, did you find that your views varied within the group?

In reality you will probably know the young people concerned and will have developed a working relationship with them so you will be able to make some judgements based on the facts of each individual concerned. For example, the 14-year-old 'babysitter' might be very capable and the teenage parent may be a mature and responsible young person who is fully aware of their responsibilities towards their baby.

Other situations could, however, require immediate action and your view of what needs to happen might not be shared by the young person.

Points for reflection

Did you know that anyone can apply for an emergency protection order for a child or young person?

Traditionally youth workers might have paid little attention to their role in the protection of children and young people, seeing this as a social worker's responsibility. Although youth workers, in common with other professional groups working with young people, receive basic training on child protection in the course of their work, this has been largely confined to raising awareness about the impact of child abuse and the procedure to follow when they know or suspect that a young person is being abused. Unless they were able to provide specific information within a case conference, or could provide evidence that could be used during the investigation stage or at a hearing, they were unlikely to be involved to any great degree during any enquiry or court proceedings. Many felt that the support they were able to offer was minimal and the situation was largely out of their hands once child protection services became involved.

Development of safeguarding policies and practices

To understand the reason for the changes in the law and the emphasis on collaboration between professionals, it is necessary to first describe the events that have led to such significantly different approaches to young people's welfare, and why safeguarding forms a key chapter in a book about youth work and the law.

It is necessary to understand the social landscape that helped drive a wedge between two professional groups; youth workers and social workers, who both profess to have principles of human rights and social justice at the heart of their professional disciplines. Each group would also argue that advocating on young people's behalf is a significant feature of their work. Yet the distinction has become more marked in the last 30 years despite these shared values and skills, so what is going on?

In understanding what sets youth work apart from other disciplines and makes it more challenging for workers to collaborate on such fundamental human rights as the right to life and the right to freedom from inhuman and degrading treatment, we need to look more closely at the historical development of social work, the methods and procedures for their intervention in family life and the expectations society places on those who engage with young people in a professional capacity.

You will undoubtedly realise from your reading on the subject as well as from well-publicised cases (Colwell, Climbié and Baby P) that terrible things happen to young people. That young people are frequently and deliberately harmed when in the care of those who should be protecting them is as profoundly shocking as it is difficult to prevent.

It became increasingly evident following enquiries into child deaths in the 1970s and 80s that professional social workers needed greater powers if they were to respond effectively in dealing with those who were thought to be ill-treating the children in their care. Social workers had borne the brunt of public condemnation for failure to intervene to protect children from dangerous as well as ineffective parenting (Colwell Inquiry, 1974). This was coupled with a greater awareness of the extent and impact of child abuse which, until then, was largely considered to be physical and resulting in injury, or emotional as a consequence of neglect. Childhood sexual abuse was considered, despite some research to the contrary, to be rare and often the consequence of psychiatric disturbance.

It has been argued that the impact of the women's movement on exposing the widespread harm caused by sexual abuse was significant. The establishment of services providing counselling and refuge to women living with domestic violence and those who had been raped or sexually assaulted began to uncover childhood sexual abuse on a much larger scale than had been previously thought. Those who could were encouraged to speak out and professionals, who had previously relied on young people disclosing their abuse at the hands of their carers, became more proactive in factoring this possibility into their assessment of risk.

This increasing public awareness of the dangers children and young people faced in their own homes led to a more interventionist approach to child protection. While the death of a child from what is euphemistically known as non-accidental injury is tragic, the public demand for retribution against social workers who were deemed to have failed in their vigilance was unrelenting during the 1970s.

The case that preceded the Children Act 1989 marked a turning point for the social work profession. It happened in Cleveland and concerned the removal of a large number of children from their homes on grounds of probable sexual abuse. The inquiry (DHSS, 1988) which followed was highly critical of the social workers involved who, acting on the advice of a paediatrician, removed children from their homes. Indeed the doctor concerned was also vilified by her professional colleagues for her contention that there was sufficient physical evidence to confirm sexual assault. There were a number of specific complaints lodged by parents but some key criticisms emerged about social workers' overzealousness in removing children and severing all contact with parents and carers.

With significant political support, the parents of the children mounted a campaign for changes to the law in order to get a better balance between parental rights and child protection. The specific issues that led to changes in the law included the following.

- The lack of routes of appeal for parents against decisions made by professionals.

- The perceived absence of any scrutiny by the courts of procedures for removing children from their homes. They were seen to rubber stamp the decisions made by social workers rather than regulate their practice.

- The length of time children could be kept in care without authorisation from the courts seemed arbitrary.

- The lack of opportunity for children to be listened to and involved in decisions that affected their lives.

The Children Act 1989, which followed many of the recommendations made by Dame Elizabeth Butler-Sloss who led the enquiry, changed the way in which children were perceived and created and embodied a new principle that was embodied in law.

When a court determines any question with respect to the upbringing of a child, the child's welfare shall be the court's paramount consideration.

(The Children Act 1989 Section 1(1)(a))

This notion of the child's welfare being paramount meant that before making any order in respect of a young person under the age of 18 the court is obliged to ask itself some key questions about the impact on the child's welfare. This is known as the welfare checklist and includes:

- the wishes of the child (if the child is old enough);

- the child's physical, emotional and educational needs;

- the likely effect on the child of a change in their life and circumstances;

- the child's age, sex, background as well as any other relevant consideration;

- any harm or risk of harm to the child;

- parental capability of meeting the needs of the child.

Furthermore, the court should only make an order in respect of a child if it is satisfied that it would be better for the child than making no order at all. It is clear that refusing to make an order is a valid option for the court. This places a greater emphasis on what applicants need to do to demonstrate that an order is necessary. For example, if the applicant has behaved unreasonably in conducting enquiries into allegations of child abuse, the court can take this into account in determining whether or not to make an order.

The Children Act was designed to ensure that the interference by the state into family life was justified and that the procedures were subject to greater scrutiny and oversight by the courts. It recognised that the removal of a child from their family home was a traumatic event and that, as such, great care should be taken to hold all parties to the decision to account.

You will note that the Children Act not just imposes duties (Section 47) on local authorities to investigate circumstances where a young person is considered to be at risk of significant harm, it also imposes duties on local authorities (Section 17) to provide support to children in need and their families. This support is not explicitly defined but may include a wide range of services to young people and to their families.

As social work became increasingly more regulated and focused on child protection, youth work began to be distinguished as a profession that concerned itself primarily with the creation of leisure opportunities. Despite being seen as a vehicle for social change it was taken less seriously as a profession, despite its different approach to working with marginalised and alienated young people. Inevitably youth workers worked with a wide range of young people who were in need of protection, but their role in safeguarding young people was less central than that of social workers. Indeed, many were seen by social workers as quasi-professional and excluded from decision-making processes. Their knowledge and expertise was considered less valuable in the role of safeguarding young people.

ACTIVITY 4.3

What role do you think youth workers play in safeguarding young people? Can you think of things youth workers might need to do to build effective working relationships with other professionals?

System failure

Unfortunately tragic events such as the death of a child throw into sharp relief the deficiencies in systems designed to protect them. The death of Victoria Climbié was such an event. The public inquiry into system failure was unprecedented. At a cost of £3.8 million the inquiry, led by Lord Laming, was granted extensive powers. It took evidence from 158 witnesses and 121 child protection experts. At over 400 pages, the inquiry report published in January 2003 made 108 recommendations for changes to the system for protecting children.

In addition to the failure by those individuals directly involved in the case to conduct proper investigation into Victoria's home circumstances or to make a correct assessment of the level of harm she was exposed to, the inquiry concluded that there were more than 12 separate opportunities for at least 25 different agencies or individuals to act in very basic ways that might have saved her life.

Despite repeated concerns being raised by professionals and members of the public, there was a massive system failure. Relationships between child protection professionals were poor. There was a lack of willingness to share information and a blatant absence of personal responsibility taken by senior managers to rectify deficiencies in the system. Figure 4.1 charts the key agencies that came into contact with Victoria Climbié since she entered the United Kingdom from France.

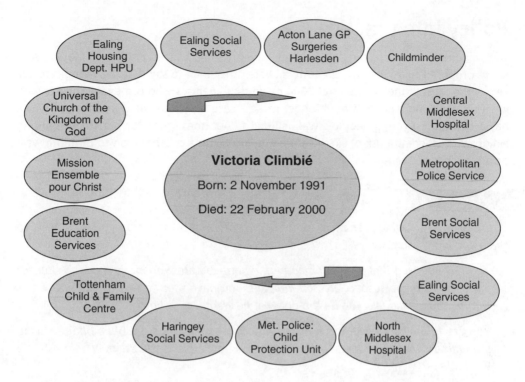

Figure 4.1 Key agencies that had contact with Victoria Climbié

The inquiry was set up in April 2001. It comprised three different statutory inquiries. You will know from Chapter 1 that this means that they were set up under Acts of Parliament. The first inquiry was established under Section 81 of the Children Act 1989 and concerned the way in which the local authority operated its children's services responsibilities. The second inquiry was established under Section 84 of the National Health Service Act 1977 to look at the role of health agencies. The third inquiry was concerned with policing and it was established under Section 49 of the Police Act 1996.

Lord Laming was given considerable latitude in determining the nature of the inquiry and decided early on that it should be public. The statutes under which the inquiries were set up gave Lord Laming the power to request the production of documents and secure testimony from witnesses and other interested parties. Delays in the production of some key documentation by Haringey Council, who had on the day of Victoria's death closed her case, resulted in the issuing of a summons under the Local Government Act to Haringey's Director of Social Services.

Suffice it to say that the breadth of the inquiry and the subsequent recommendations had a significant bearing on child protection policy and on the creation of new legal duties to cooperate to promote children's wellbeing.

Policy into practice

You will undoubtedly cover in detail aspects of *Every Child Matters* and *Youth Matters* so it is not proposed to go into any great detail here other than to say that the changes to the law in the form of the Children Act 2004 mean that agencies who come into contact with young people and families can no longer make a case for withholding information which has a bearing on young people's wellbeing. The Act goes much further than requiring action when there is a risk of significant harm and expects collaboration to promote well-being in a positive sense.

ACTIVITY **4.4**

Consider the following scenarios and ask yourself what information you may need to share and with whom.

1. *You have noticed that a young man with whom you are working is showing signs of injuries which you suspect are self-inflicted. You have tried to talk to him about this but he refuses and tells you he can do what he wants to his body.*

2. *You are told by a 14-year-old female that she was filmed on a mobile phone having sex with another young person and that she is upset this footage is now being shared with others.*

3. *A young woman has confided in you that she plans to run away from home to escape a marriage her family has arranged for her in Pakistan.*

Accountability under the Children Act 2004

In addition to the duty to cooperate and to create a database of information on children and young people, the Act also vested formal personal liability for children's welfare in a Director of, and a lead councillor for, Children's Services (Sections 18 and 19 of the Children Act 2004) in every local authority. In December 2008, following the public inquiry into the death of a child known as Baby P, Haringey once again came under the spotlight for their failure to take preventative action to protect a child and the resultant removal of the Director of Children's Services provides an illustration of just what personal accountability means.

Liability for failure to disclose information that safeguards a young person

Just as a youth worker is expected to do all they can to bring concerns they have about a young person to the attention of those who have the authority to act, it is worth noting that failure to do so can give rise to a breach of the young person's human rights.

From our earlier chapter on human rights law, you will have seen that failure to protect young people could find the organisation you work for in breach of Article 3 of the

European Convention which concerns inhuman and degrading treatment (*Z* v. *UK*, 2002 34 EHRR 3). The case of Z had gone first to the House of Lords who had rejected Z's claim against the local authority for failing to protect him and his siblings from sustained abuse in childhood. It had taken the local authority five years from the first of several reports to social services about the family before they acted. The European Court held that the state had been in breach of their obligations to protect the children from ill-treatment of which it had, or ought to have had, knowledge.

Clearly when a baby or young child dies at the hand of a parent or carer there is a justifiable outcry, but there are many circumstances that youth workers will be faced with when a young person's welfare is seriously compromised, and they find it more difficult to persuade other agencies to respond. Indeed when the young person is older, they might be seen by some people to be partly responsible for what is happening to them. Many people hold beliefs about young people's culpability that are dangerous and will need to be challenged if we are to help young people make the difficult transition into adulthood safely.

However, there is growing awareness of the different risks faced by young people and, increasingly, parliament is legislating to give effect to the protection it affords young people as it responds to emerging information about the different risks young people face.

One example of this is the Forced Marriage (Civil Protection) Act 2007, which gives the court the power to make Forced Marriage Protection Orders and to attach powers of arrest for their breach. The legislation passed through its various stages in record time because it had the support of all three main political parties as well as that of grass roots organisations working with ethnic minority young women. The powers to intervene extend to third parties who are able to apply for an injunction on a young person's behalf.

C H A P T E R   R E V I E W

- The Children Act 1989 introduced the welfare principle and required courts to treat it as paramount when making decisions about whether or not to make an order.

- The Children Act 1989 provides a framework for investigation into a child's circumstances, for providing support to the child and their family, for considering where the child will live, with whom and for how long.

- *Every Child Matters* and *Youth Matters* outline the government's policy on integration of services for children and young people, and were developed as a direct result of the recommendations from the Victoria Climbié Inquiry.

- The Children Act 2004 created a duty to cooperate to promote the wellbeing of children and vested strategic accountability for children's welfare in Directors of Children's Services and lead members for Children's Services.

- A failure to act to protect a young person may constitute a breach of their human rights.

- There is increasing awareness that children can be exposed to a wide range of risks from those who are responsible for their care and parliament continues to implement legislation to reduce the risk.

FURTHER READING

Fortin, J (2003) *Children's rights and the developing law*. London: LexisNexis.

REFERENCES

National Health Service Act 1977. London: HMSO.

Children Act 1989. London: HMSO.

Every child matters Green Paper 2003. London: The Stationery Office.

Children Act 2004. London: The Stationery Office.

Youth matters Green Paper 2005. London: The Stationery Office.

Forced Marriage (Civil Protection) Act 2007. London: The Stationery Office.

Butler-Sloss, E (1988) *Report of the inquiry into child abuse in Cleveland 1987*. London: HMSO.

Committee of inquiry into the care and supervision provided in relation to Maria Colwell 1974. London: HMSO.

Fortin, J (2003) *Children's rights and the developing law*. London: LexisNexis.

Laming, Lord (2003) *The Victoria Climbié inquiry: report of an inquiry by Lord Laming*. London: Department of Health.

Chapter 5
Mental health

CHAPTER OBJECTIVES

By the end of this chapter you should be able to:

- understand the relationship between young people's mental health, their capacity to make decisions and the protection available to those who become ill;

- critically reflect on mental health policy, practice and the legislative framework in the UK, particularly the Mental Health Act 1983 and Mental Health Act 2007;

- identify what role the professional youth worker has in supporting young people whose mental health is compromised and in optimising young people's opportunities to enjoy good mental health;

- relate your knowledge to the National Occupational Standards 2.1 and 2.2 which concern young people's entitlements and rights to mental wellbeing.

In this chapter we will build on some of the ideas introduced in the previous chapters and examine more closely how poor mental health impacts adversely on young people's enjoyment of their basic human rights. It should enhance your ability to contribute to the early detection and support for young people who are experiencing mental health difficulties, particularly as early intervention is recognised (Wright *et al.*, 2006) as having a beneficial effect on outcomes for young people in the longer term.

You might have some experience of different methods of delivering early preventative services or, given the prevalence of mental health problems, it would be rather more surprising if you did not have some personal experience to draw on, either because you have used mental health services or you know someone who has. As high-profile public figures have disclosed their struggles with mental illness, we could be entering a new era where mental ill health does not have the same stigma as it once did. If so it will inevitably benefit young people at a time where specific types of mental health problems such as eating disorders appear to be on the increase.

ACTIVITY 5.1

As you are probably well aware, there is a fairly diverse range of topics that might be covered in a chapter on mental health. Work with colleagues to list some of these to see if you can begin to define mental health.

Did you begin with a list of positive features such as emotional wellbeing, or did you find that you began to make a list of the different types of conditions or disorders, such as depression, schizophrenia, attention deficit hyperactivity disorder (ADHD) and bipolar disorder (or manic depression)? It is little wonder that we struggle to think of mental health as a positive concept given that mental *health* services generally describe the type of professional help that is only accessed when people are ill.

It should not surprise you to find that this chapter will not only focus on what happens when things begin to go wrong for young people and how professional youth workers might respond, but we will begin to examine the basis on which some types of mental health disorders are classified and question what this means for young people's human rights and autonomy in their progression towards adulthood.

This means that we will not just look at how best we can respond to help the young person overcome their emotional and psychological difficulties, but whether a diagnosis is helpful to young people's sense of their own value or self-worth or how they are perceived by others.

For, unlike most other areas of health where there is dependence on the consent of the subject themselves in order for treatment to take place, professionals involved in mental health services are often called upon to treat young people against their will. This could include involuntary detention as well as involuntary treatment, so the safeguards that need to be in place have to be sufficiently robust to protect vulnerable young people from arbitrary invasion of their bodily integrity and to ensure that they are able to recover from their experience and enjoy healthy productive lives, even after they have been deprived of the freedom to choose for themselves whether or not to accept treatment.

You will remember from Chapter 3 that treatment without consent is potentially a battery and that consent is therefore required before a Fraser-competent young person can be treated. In *Re R*, the courts were concerned to enable treatment to be given to administer anti-psychotic drugs to a young woman who, during intermittent periods of lucidity, was refusing treatment. In this case the local authority applied for the young woman to be made a ward of court to enable the court to 'consent' on her behalf.

Similarly in *Re W*, also discussed in the chapter on consent, the court used its inherent jurisdiction to override the refusal of treatment by a young woman who had the eating disorder anorexia nervosa. Lord Donaldson, in his judgment, described the court's authority to invoke its inherent jurisdiction as one that does *not do so by ordering the doctors to treat which even within the court's powers, would be an abuse of them, or by ordering the minor to accept treatment, but by authorising doctors to treat the minor in accordance with their clinical judgment, subject to any restrictions which the court may impose.* It might be difficult to see the distinction being made here between authorising treatment and ordering the young person to accept it, but it offers the clinician some immunity from claims for battery. There is clearly an assumption that doctors will act properly when exercising clinical judgement about treatment.

The court's reasoning in *Re W* was interesting insofar as they were willing to classify anorexia as a mental health problem which affected capacity, because they accepted that the control being exercised by the selective refusal of treatment by the young woman was a feature of anorexia and therefore went to the very heart of her inability to reason.

ACTIVITY **5.2**

How easy is it to distinguish between the types of controlling behaviours that might be described as irrational compulsions and those that might seem irrational but are deeply held beliefs? Does it matter how widespread the belief?

Imagine a situation where a young woman, who attends your centre, begins to describe visions she has had of spirits, both good and evil. She is able to describe in detail the images she sees and the conversations she has had with these spirits. For the most part she is happy to hear these voices but describes being overwhelmed and at times frightened by them.

Hearing voices is one of the symptoms associated with mental health problems, is she therefore ill?

Would your response differ if the names she gave these spirits accorded with your own beliefs?

Within your professional role you are likely to come across situations where you are using your judgement in determining when to seek further specialist help from mental health practitioners. How you respond is likely to be affected by your own values and beliefs, either about the rationality of the young person's reasoning or your confidence in the type of treatment on offer. It is important that you are able to identify when your own beliefs affect your response to young people's emotional needs.

Current research suggests that the earlier the intervention and treatment, the better the longer term outcome. Yet we also know that the threshold for accessing specialist mental health services can appear very high and you might have to find alternative ways to address the difficulties young people face, for example, through developing your own counselling skills or group work. You might, additionally, want to develop closer working relationships with mental health practitioners and consider opportunities for joint working. Within the extended schools programme there are more opportunities for co-located services that you would want to explore.

The benefit of joint working, in order to provide seamless support to young people, is fairly well documented. A study by Shucksmith *et al.* (2006) examined co-location of professional support services in schools and found that although it provided easier access in a familiar environment to the young people who were experiencing mental health problems, the impact on teacher's own understanding and behaviour was minimal. The findings suggested that teachers ultimately preferred to learn from other teachers than to take the opportunity to learn from working with colleagues from different professional backgrounds.

As youth workers you are likely to be working with colleagues who do not share your perspective or work within the same professional framework, but you can see from the National Occupational Standards on Youth Work that there is considerable scope for you to consider what your role is in managing interprofessional relationships, so that they don't get in the way of providing high-quality provision for young people.

Prevalence of mental health problems among young people

Because mental health is so fundamental to our effective functioning and because of the prevalence of mental ill health among young people, it might be useful to consider what background statistics tell us about the different and most common types of conditions which are classified, within both the 5–16 and the 16–19 age ranges, as mental health problems.

It is estimated (Office of National Statistics, 2004) that, of the 8.8 million 5–16 year olds in the UK, almost ten per cent have a mental disorder. Around 600,000 young people between 16 and 19 years old have a mental health problem. If we consider the hidden nature of self-harm, including eating disorders, compared with official figures, this is likely to be significantly higher. It is not hard to understand the significance for professionals working with young people if one in five over 16 year olds are at risk. Many of those affected talk of their isolation. You are likely to want to review your youth work strategy as well as your practice to ensure that young people at risk or recovering from mental illness are able to access safe and welcoming services so critical to their recovery.

Almost half a million young people with mental health problems are between 11 and 16 years old. Within this group about 6.6 per cent are diagnosed with a conduct disorder. While it is difficult for researchers to identify simple and singular factors that contribute towards children's development, it is argued (Rutter and Giller, 1983) that adverse parenting practice, poverty, neglect and low parental expectations of school are related and cumulatively more likely to predispose children to criminality.

There is certainly a higher proportion of young people involved in the criminal justice system who have a diagnosable mental health problem, but does this mean that disordered conduct leads to later criminal behaviour, or that the factors that predispose young people to poor mental health are the same factors that are present among young people who have offended? The following section will examine the relationship between conduct and diagnosis.

The problem with behaviour

You are likely to have encountered a diverse range of perspectives about conduct disorders and you might have your own views on them but one of the most controversial mental illnesses among young people is that of attention deficit hyperactivity disorder (ADHD)

ADHD is classified as a psychiatric disorder in the American and Statistical Manual of Mental Disorders (1994). The distinction between ADHD and ADD is the presence of hyperactivity. This is characterised by a lack of impulse control and an apparent absence of concern for the consequences of actions. The characteristics of impulsivity, hyperactivity and inattentiveness, arguably present to some extent in a great majority of developing human beings, began to take shape as discrete medical phenomena in the early part of the last century. Initially attributed to minimal brain damage the discovery, in the mid-1930s, of the effects of psycho-stimulant medication in reducing levels of activity and restlessness appeared to confirm that these characteristics were, indeed, biochemical in origin.

The ADHD debate has become increasingly polarised: some argue that the characteristics displayed by children who are identified as having conduct disorders are biological in origin, with a proportion of those finding a genetic link, whereas others remain sceptical about attempts to find a genetic predisposition to ADHD. There is, for example, no physical 'test' for ADHD. Evidence needed for a diagnosis is subjective: based on observation of behaviour and assessment of performance on a number of different tasks undertaken in different environments.

Many respected authors recognise that its aetiology is likely to be a combination of all three. It is generally, although not universally, considered to be a disorder peculiar to children and young people. The diagnostic criteria stipulate that symptoms must be extreme in relation to the age and gender of the young person, persistent, pervasive and evident in pre-seven year olds.

ADHD is controversial for two reasons the first of which is the ascribing of a mental health diagnosis to what is essentially a set of subjectively assessed behaviours. Some critics have suggested that the behaviours may themselves be normal responses to different situations and external stimuli.

Gordon and Barkley (1999) question the general failure to take seriously the non-specific nature of inattention, pointing out that:

> *Some variant of inattention (poor concentration, distractibility, disorganization, failure to complete task, absentmindedness, etc.) can emerge as a feature in any number of psychiatric, educational and medical circumstances – from substance abuse, schizophrenia, depression and anxiety to migraine headaches, boredom and unrecognized cognitive limitations . . . its presence alone does little to narrow the range of diagnostic possibilities.*

(*ADHD Report* 7.5, pages 1–8)

Others point to a correlation between diet and behaviour. It is certainly true that there is an increase in reported numbers of children and young people from poorer socioeconomic backgrounds who have an ADHD diagnosis. What is less clear is whether those things we associate with poverty, such as lack of access to affordable nutrition and low aspirations, cause mental ill health or exacerbate it. Recent research (Sayce and Morris, 1999) points to social inequality as a major determinant of poor mental health. There is a greater level of mental illness in societies where there is a wide gap between those who are rich and those who are poor than there is in societies where most people are very poor.

Early research into ADHD showed a high correlation between childhood conduct problems and maternal depression. During this time it was also discovered that prescribing amphetamines had a marked effect on controlling the symptoms. This is the second reason why the ADHD diagnosis is so controversial. There is widespread debate, which is outside the scope of this book, on the ethics and efficacy of prescribing methylphenidate (Ritalin), the most widely used pharmacological treatment, to young people. It could be argued that where there is a pre-existing mental health problem within the family, clinicians are likely to lean towards prescribing drugs to manage the young person's symptoms rather than take a longer term approach to behaviour management. If true, this may be partly due to the level of commitment and compliance needed by families, schools and other professionals to working together on such a programme. You might have your own views on this.

Over the last 15 years in the UK, successive government initiatives designed to address antisocial behaviour have included parenting programmes as part of a bank of interventions designed to modify young people's behaviour. Although there is evidence that effective parenting programmes can have a significant and positive impact on family functioning, many parents feel that they are being blamed for their child's behaviour. It is possible that the 'blame' attached to conduct disorders creates an effect whereby parents are more likely to pursue a diagnosis which then shifts the blame from the parent to the condition itself.

There is a real danger that in some circumstances schools, parents and children themselves can become overly reliant on finding a medical cause for, and solution to, their child's behaviour. ADHD, with the blessing of the medical profession, which is as susceptible as other, including legal, professions to cultural, racial and gender-based assumptions about normality is a convenient psychiatric label with which to explain a young person's behaviour.

The more successful approaches to managing and treating ADHD are those that recognise and target multiple factors; those that combine advice and support on parenting with additional support in schools, changes in diet, as well as creating opportunities for young people to express themselves. Child psychiatrist Sami Timimi (2002), for example, argues that prescribing drugs might be helpful in the short term but their main function should be to give everyone concerned some respite which can then help restore energy and help support the transition to a more integrated approach.

CASE STUDY

Jamilla is a 13-year-old pupil at a school where you are based. She has a Special Educational Needs (SEN) plan based on her ADHD diagnosis. There is a review of the plan and she wants you to represent her at the meeting.

The head of year is proposing that she be moved to a 'special school' which can better meet her educational needs. She has been in trouble on a number of occasions, answering back and being disruptive in some classes. She has additional support for some lessons, but not others. Her support teacher usually sits at the back of the class marking homework until she is needed to escort Jamilla to the head's office.

Jamilla's mother, who also has mental health problems, is hoping to get to the meeting but Jamilla is afraid that even if she does attend she will not be confident enough to represent her.

- *What sort of things might you want to do before you attend?*

- *What further information do you need in order to marshal your arguments?*

- *Who else might you involve?*

Children with SEN are particularly vulnerable to being excluded from school because of their behaviour (Fortin, 2006) and the extent that different schools pick up on underlying difficulties is variable. The House of Lords has confirmed in *Phelps* v. *London Borough of Hillingdon*, that if educational practitioners fail to exercise skill and care in the delivery of educational provision appropriate to the needs of young people with special educational needs, the local authority can be held liable in negligence.

Young people and psychiatric disorders

Giving a diagnosis of mental illness has profound implications for individuals, particularly when they are young. While medical treatments for physical conditions invariably depend on the consent of the patient or the overriding 'welfare' principle when capacity is at issue, psychiatric disturbance is likely to presume an absence of capacity. Consequently, the best interests of the patient are determined by professionals in conjunction with those who have parental responsibility, rather than imposing a duty to take into account the independent and potentially competing viewpoint of the child.

We have already examined some of the options available to parents, the courts and doctors when seeking to treat a young person against their wishes when they become dangerously ill. The system of using different methods to admit, detain and treat young people who become very ill has been somewhat modified by the Mental Health Act 2007, which received Royal Assent in July 2007. It introduced greater safeguards for 16 and 17 year olds, who have the capacity to consent but do not do so, to admission, detention or treatment on the basis of parental consent. The 2007 Act also requires the hospital manager to ensure that the young person's environment is suitable for a person of their age.

The changes strike a better balance between the ECHR (Article 5) freedom from arbitrary detention and the rights of the parents (Article 8) to respect for family life. One of the concerns raised in the Council of Europe (2000) report was that protective measures for young people being detained and treated needed to be more stringent than for adult patients. Although available for all those who are mentally ill, the Mental Health Act 1983 is less frequently used for the detention and treatment of young people. This is because of the perceived stigma of being sectioned (Section 2). Unfortunately most young people are unaware of the strict legislative safeguards it provides compared with the unregulated system of voluntary admission.

ACTIVITY **5.3**

Consider the advantages and disadvantages of treating young people under the Mental Health Act 1983.

Overall do you think the advantages outweigh the disadvantages?

Does the recognition of mental illness as a disability (Disability Discrimination Act 2005) make it more or less likely that the stigmatising effect of treatment under mental health legislation is no longer relevant?

Jane Fortin (2006) argues persuasively that the scope for coercion by those with parental responsibility (including the local authority) applied to secure a young person's 'voluntary' admission is unfair. When this is coupled with the methods used to detain a young person against their wishes, such as removal of outdoor clothes or use of tranquilising medication, it is likely to breach human rights legislation. She argues that the 1997 decision in *R v. Kirklees MBC*, which concerned the detention of a 12 year old, in hospital nightwear on an adult ward, could be challenged under Article 3 which prohibits inhuman or degrading treatment.

It is imperative that the level of scrutiny over decisions and powers that impact upon the autonomy of young people with a diagnosed psychiatric illness is sufficiently robust. It is in this area that the law has been most active in overriding the wishes of the child and resorting to the more paternalistic 'best interests' test by substituting its own judgment as to what treatment should legitimately be given to a reluctant patient.

The law relating to young people's mental health is arbitrary and, therefore, can leave the professional youth worker confused as to how they should advise a young person. On the one hand, young people should be encouraged to weigh up the options and make choices, but on the other, the law would seem to want to maintain the right to override their decisions if practitioners consider them to be irrational.

For children and young people with conduct disorders the issues may be even less clear. They might feel as though they have little right to refuse treatment, particularly if by taking medication they conform to the expectations adults have of them and calm down.

In addition to the involuntary treatment of those who are mentally ill there are, according to Mason and McCall Smith (1999), the associated powers of detention which, in a society governed by the rule of law, is a role generally reserved for the judiciary.

The inconsistency and lack of agreement among medics about the existence and prevalence of ADHD is extremely confusing, not just for other professionals concerned with children's health and welfare – teachers, social workers and allied professionals within the fields of community safety and criminal justice – but for children who are diagnosed with the disorder and their families. It is probable that only a proportion of parents and child care professionals will be able to access and, furthermore, make sense of the plethora of research and opinion that surrounds ADHD in order to make informed decisions that are genuinely in the best interests of the child.

C H A P T E R   R E V I E W

- The prevalence of mental ill health in young adolescents is high, with official statistics suggesting that one in five young people between 13 and 19 have a mental health problem.

- Conduct disorders feature among the most controversial of mental health problems, with widely divergent views on their diagnosis and management.

- Changes in mental health legislation through the Mental Health Act 2007 provide greater safeguards for 16 and 17 year olds but do not expand the protection offered to young people under the age of 16.

- Hospital managers are required under the 2007 Act, to ensure the hospital environment is suitable for the age of the young person.

- Young people who are admitted, detained and treated under the Mental Health Act 1983 have greater protection than those who are 'voluntarily' patients, who have to rely on the Human Rights Act to challenge their detention and treatment.

- Mental health, subject to certain criteria, might now come within the ambit of the Disability Discrimination Act.

FURTHER READING

American Psychiatric Association (2000) *Diagnostic and statistical manual of mental disorders,* 4th edn. Washington, DC: American Psychiatric Publishing.

Boris, M and Mandel, FS (1994) Food and additives are common causes for the Attention Deficit/Hyperactive Disorder in children. *Annals of Allergy,* 72: 462–68.

Council of Europe (2000) *White Paper regarding a draft recommendation on legal protection of persons suffering from mental disorder especially those placed as involuntary patients.* Strasbourg: Council of Europe.

Gordon, M and Barkley, RA (1999) Is all inattention ADD/ADHD? *ADHD Report,* 7.5: 1–8.

Hughes, L (1999) How professionals perceive ADHD, in Cooper, P and Bilton, K (eds) *ADHD: research, practice and opinion.* New York: Wiley (pages 187–88).

Mason, JK and McCall Smith, A (1999) *Law and medical ethics.* London: Butterworths.

NICE (2000) *Methylphenidate (Ritalin/Equasym) for attention deficit hyperactivity disorder (ADHD).* London: National Institute for Clinical Excellence.

ONS (2004) *The mental health of children and adolescents in Great Britain.* London: Office of National Statistics.

Sayce, L and Morris, D (1999) *Outsiders coming in: achieving social inclusion for people with mental health problems.* London: Mind.

Timimi, S (2002) *Pathological child psychiatry and the medicalization of childhood.* Hove: Brunner-Routledge.

Wright, A, McGorry, PD and Harris, MG (2006) Development and evaluation of a youth mental health community awareness campaign – The Compass Strategy. *BMC Public Health,* 2006.6 (215): 22.

WEBSITES

www.youngminds.org

www.direct.gov.uk

www.worldhealthorganisation.com

www.mk-adhd.org.uk

REFERENCES

Mental Health Act 1983. London: Department of Health.

Disability Discrimination Act 1995. London: The Stationery Office.

Mental Health Act 2007. London: The Stationery Office.

Fortin, J (2006) *Children's rights and the developing law.* London: LexisNexis.

Gordon, M and Barkley, RA (1999) Is all inattention ADD/ADHD? *ADHD Report* 7.5: 1–8.

Mason, JK and McCall Smith, A (1999) *Law and medical ethics.* London: Butterworths.

ONS (2004) *The mental health of children and adolescents in Great Britain.* London: Office of National Statistics.

Rutter, M and Giller, H (1983) *Juvenile delinquency: trends and perspectives.* New York: Penguin.

Sayce, L and Morris, D (1999) *Outsiders coming in: achieving social inclusion for people with mental health problems.* London: Mind.

Shucksmith, K, Spratt, J, Philip, K and Watson, C (2006) Interpersonal support of mental wellbeing in schools: a Bourdieuan perspective. *Journal of Interprofessional Care*, 20 (4): 391–402.

Timimi, S (2002) *Pathological child psychiatry and the medicalization of childhood.* Hove: Brunner-Routledge.

Wright, A, McGorry, PD and Harris, MG (2006) Development and evaluation of a youth mental health community awareness campaign – The Compass Strategy. *BMC Public Health*, 2006.6 (215): 22.

CASES

Phelps v. *London Borough of Hillingdon* [2001] 2AC 619.

R v. *Kirklees MBC ex p C* [1997] 2 FLR 180.

Re R [1992] Fam 11, (1992) 7 BMLR 147.

Re W (A Minor) (Medical Treatment: Court's Jurisdiction [1993] 1FLR 1).

Chapter 6
Crime and disorder

CHAPTER OBJECTIVES

By the end of this chapter you should be able to:

• understand the approach taken at a national and local policy level to addressing crime and antisocial behaviour among young people;

• understand the legislative framework and the system as it relates to young people and antisocial behaviour;

• appreciate the difference between risk factors and causal factors in predicting areas and populations in which to target preventative work with young people;

• understand the relationship between different professional bodies and their approaches to dealing with crime and disorder in the community;

• consider what lessons we can draw from inquiries into crimes committed against children and young people in order to determine what role the professional youth worker needs to take.

During the 1990s there was a good deal of public demand for the government to crack down on what was widely perceived to be increasing lawlessness among young people. In 1993, the conviction of two ten year olds for the murder of two-year-old James Bulger not only caused national outrage but marked the beginning of the end of the assumption in law that ten year olds should be protected from the full force of the criminal law. Although the European Commission decided against the UK in 1999 over the fairness of the way the trial had been conducted, it concluded that this did not amount to *inhuman and degrading* treatment. The appetite among the British public was, however, for greater levels of control over the behaviour of children and young people.

The end of the decade saw the creation of a major new piece of legislation which has had a profound impact on the lives of children and young people and, according to most children's rights commentators, has led to the development of the most draconian system of juvenile justice in Europe.

The new law created a crime and disorder reduction partnership in every local authority area to share intelligence and coordinate a response to crime and antisocial behaviour, and a Youth Justice Board to oversee a dedicated youth offending service with a key role in preventing young people from offending. It abolished the rule, known as *doli incapax*, which placed on the prosecution the responsibility for demonstrating that young people between the ages of 10 and 13 had capacity necessary to establish criminal intent. It is, however, for the creation of ASBOs that the Crime and Disorder Act 1998 is better known.

Given all these changes, you could be forgiven for wondering why a chapter on crime and disorder is located towards the end of a book about law and youth work rather than occupying a more prominent position. This is because despite public perception, exacerbated by media treatment such as the 'shop a yob' campaigns run by *The Sun* newspaper, the number of young people who are involved in crime is relatively small. Research undertaken by Women in Journalism in 2008 found that 85 per cent of the 1000 boys questioned in a survey believed that they were negatively portrayed by the media. This research considered media stories about young people and showed that of the roughly 8,500 stories about teenage boys in national and regional newspapers run over the previous year over half were about crime: *the word most commonly used to describe them was 'yobs' (591 times), followed by 'thugs' (254 times), 'sick' (119 times) and 'feral' (96 times).* The research concluded that the best chance a teenager had of receiving sympathetic coverage was if they died.

In comparison to those who are exposed to harm, neglect and persistent bullying (often considered to be low level, but frequently accompanied by criminal acts such as robbery, battery and harassment), the number of young people who offend is fairly low. It is recognised that the many young people exposed to violence in the home and those who are neglected as a result of parental alcohol and substance misuse are often the hidden victims of crime.

It is, however, notoriously difficult to obtain accurate statistics on children who are victims of crime. Crimes are generally compiled by type of offence rather than age of victim, although the government announced its intention through the Youth Crime Action Plan 2008 to extend the British Crime Survey to under 16s for the first time to help quantify the number of young victims more accurately. The statistics on young people who have crimes committed against them, who witness crimes, and who are adversely affected by crime in their communities, are unreliable at present. Anecdotal information from young people themselves suggests that anxiety about levels of crime is very high among them, and the impact of being bombarded with messages about the risks posed by other young people makes it difficult for them to form relationships with other young people. Research (Morgan, 1988) has shown that acquiring the status of victim is more difficult if you are young. Some local authority areas (Hull and Bolton) have child witness support schemes to enable young people to have additional psychological support should they witness crime, but these schemes are few and far between. With levels of witness intimidation being quite high in some areas of the UK, it will come as little surprise to youth work professionals that young people's confidence in the criminal justice system itself is low. Similarly, systems for recording the follow-up action taken with young people living with domestic violence is variable, despite the emphasis through government policy of keeping young people safe. The latest report by Lord Laming (March 2009) cites the relationships between different professionals as being a major factor in reducing the risk of a young person becoming a victim of crime.

Links between being a victim and becoming involved in offending

Not only is exposure to crime harmful to young people's safety and wellbeing, but there is some evidence to suggest that some types of crimes might make a young person more susceptible to future offending. You may well be wary, as are many professionals working directly with young people, of making such a huge leap, but there is a huge interest among policy makers and professionals in finding ways of preventing offending and targeting scarce resources more effectively. Consequently much research has focused on finding common sets of factors among the existing population of offenders, to see if it is possible to predict with any degree of accuracy which young people are at highest risk. These are known as predictive risk factors.

The research (Smith and Allen, 2004) shows the strongest link between being the victim of assault with a weapon and robbery and future offending. Those who had experienced repeat victimisation presented as being at significantly greater risk.

ACTIVITY *6.1*

- *What other factors do you think might increase the risk of future offending? Discuss with colleagues and see how many you agree on.*

- *Do you believe that targeting interventions at young people who present with more than one risk factor is justified?*

Did you find this activity useful? Many youth workers and youth work academics have raised concerns about undertaking targeted intervention work with young people, arguing that this goes against the ethos of youth work. You may have found wildly divergent opinions among the group about both the ethics and the usefulness of identifying risk factors.

Predicting future offending

It is widely understood that there are categories of risk that have greater predictive value than others, and that presenting with a number of the risk factors incrementally increases the risk of poor outcomes, including involvement in offending. The different risks are presented in Table 6.1.

It is generally understood that the higher the number of predictive risk factors the greater the likelihood of becoming involved in offending. In 2007 the charity 4Children found that of young people in custody almost half had been in care and nearly three-quarters had been excluded from school at some point. Therefore, it might be suggested that establishing risk factors helps to target preventative interventions more effectively.

Targeting young people on the basis of a set of risk factors is not only contentious but it is also misleading. To focus simply on risks that are present, albeit to a greater extent in some of the most disadvantaged communities and among some marginalised groups of

Table 6.1 Predictive risk factors for future offending

Domain	Risk Factors
Family	• Low income and poor housing • Single parenthood • Family conflict • Family member involved in criminality • Poor parental supervision
School	• Poor attendance and exclusion • Low attainment • Poor school environment • Disruptive or aggressive behaviour
Community	• Neighbourhood neglect • High levels of criminal damage • High levels of drug use
Peer	• Associating with other young people who commit crimes • Bullying • Use of substances including alcohol

young people, can have a stigmatising effect. You might argue that these factors are present across the wider population and yet most people do not commit crime. The research has, after all, focused on finding common features among a population of offenders and is, therefore, not reflective of the wider group of vulnerable young people who live crime-free lives. Therefore, it is important to recognise that these are *risk* factors not *causal* factors. Recent research commissioned by the Joseph Rowntree Trust (Anderson *et al.*, 2009) has questioned the ethics of using ONSET, the Youth Justice Board's assessment tool for determining risk, and of the storage, access and sharing of this type of information.

Public policy has seen a shift towards protective factors; those attributes and interventions that reduce the impact of risk factors. This means that even when risks are established the focus should be on building in protective factors such as social and emotional skills, positive adult influences, particularly positive parenting, and educational attainment. They are considered to significantly reduce the potentially negative consequences of poor home, school and peer influences on young people.

This has formed the basis of government policy on early preventative programmes for young people over the last ten years. Programmes such as *Sure Start* for under 5s, the *Children's Fund* for 5–13 year olds and *Connexions* for 13–19 year olds have been further supplemented by the *Positive Activities for Young People* programme aimed at 8–19 year olds at risk of social exclusion and community crime.

Feinstein (2009) argues in a paper on using sport and leisure activities, that interventions need to be structured if they are to be effective and the evaluation team reviewing the effectiveness of prevention services in the National Evaluation of Children's Fund Programme (2006) suggested that where services are targeted at whole populations, such as school year groups or whole schools, they are likely to be more effective at addressing the problem as they do not 'miss' children who do not meet all the criteria, do not harm those who are at low risk and are preferable from an ethical point of view insofar as they are less stigmatising. There is increasing recognition that positive parenting programmes, provided they are offered as an early protective measure, can be very helpful in restoring good relationships between parents and young people. Findings show that the greatest benefits come from addressing parenting with pre-school and nursery age children, but there are also some good examples of parenting programmes aimed at teenagers as well as those parents of young people who present with behavioural disorders in primary school.

Whatever your point of view, increasingly government programmes such as RESPECT and *Aiming High for Young People* advocate more integrated approaches to reducing crime and antisocial behaviour, combining support, conflict resolution and diversionary activities alongside parenting advice in order to address the multiple predictive risk factors associated with crime and antisocial behaviour.

McHugh (2008), in an article for the National Youth Association, challenges the idea that youth work is a vehicle for creating diversion among the young people who hang about on the streets, arguing that: *as a collective of workers we would probably struggle to alter the course of the crime and disorder based youth work policies of this epoch. Yet we can alter how we work within the constraints of these policies, we do not have to be the overseers in the 'Positive Activities . . .' plantation. We can be the catalyst for emancipation.*

CASE STUDY

Jade is 14. She and her ten-year-old brother Mal live with their mother in a house they rent from the council. Mal is well known to the neighbours for being a 'bit wild' and 'hard to manage'. He is often seen by neighbours causing damage to their fencing and throwing stones at cats. One neighbour has complained to the council.

Jade spends her evenings hanging around with a group of young people in the local park at the weekend and in the evenings. They sometimes drink alcohol and can be fairly rowdy. Parents of other younger children don't like using the play area when they are around mainly because of their swearing.

You may consider the activities described in the case study above as insufficiently severe to demand the full force of the law, yet there are a wide range of powers available to the police and local authority, including the police power to confiscate alcohol from the young people and the local authority power to seek possession of the family home should all other efforts to control the behaviour be ineffective.

The National Occupational Standards on Youth Work, discussed in Chapter 1, cite a role for the youth worker in promoting young people's self-awareness (Section 1.3) and in engaging with the local community (Section 3.2). You might have some ideas about how to do this but it is worth understanding what the provisions of the Crime and Disorder Act mean for young people, and how the law has progressed since 1998.

We discussed in Chapter 4 some of the powers the local authority has, through its children's services, to investigate circumstances where children and young people are at risk of harm. In this chapter we will examine the wide range of powers the local authority and the police have to deal with antisocial behaviour, before considering what role, if any, the youth worker might play in relation to either of the young people.

Crime and Disorder Act 1998

The Crime and Disorder Act 1998 defines antisocial behaviour as:

> *Acting in a manner that caused, or was likely to cause harassment, alarm or distress to one or more persons, not of the same household as [the perpetrator].*

It is a fairly broad definition and is recognised as being difficult to accurately measure given that it can include such passive activities as hanging around or playing ball to criminal activity such as criminal damage and harassment. Records on its prevalence are inaccurate unless the behaviour is actually criminal, as the recording of low-level nuisance complaints is variable across local authority areas. Another way of measuring levels of antisocial behaviour is to undertake surveys on community perceptions of antisocial behaviour. This is also likely to vary according to the levels of tolerance among different communities and to the confidence members of the public have in the authorities' ability to address the problem. Members of the public, although they might be fearful of groups of young people hanging around, also frequently express concern about the lack of available provision.

If we consider the case study above it becomes clear that the behaviour exhibited by both young people comes within the scope of this Act. However, only Mal's behaviour has generated an actual complaint. He is only ten years old and therefore comes within the scope of the Crime and Disorder Act.

The Act introduced the ASBO (Section 1). An application by the police or the local authority can be made to the magistrates' court. Mal does not have to have been convicted of a crime in order for the application to be made. There is, therefore, no requirement to meet the criminal standard of proof. Instead, the applicant needs only to satisfy the court that on a *balance of probability* (the civil standard) the criteria for issuing an order have been met. However, this in itself is fairly contentious, as breaching the order could lead to much harsher penalties; those that are normally reserved for activities that meet the higher criminal standard. Civil libertarians have expressed considerable disquiet about the erosion of our civil liberties through attaching criminal penalties to the breaching of an order which does not, during the initial application, have to satisfy the criminal standard of proof.

ASBOs can and do prohibit a very wide range of behaviours, including the types of clothing a young person can wear, their association with others and their freedom to enter defined geographical areas.

ASBOs are used to different degrees in different local authority areas, with some local authorities and the police adopting a zero tolerance approach whereas others have been less willing to apply for ASBOs. Much has been written about their usefulness and it is not proposed to go into these arguments in any detail here; suffice it to say they are widely criticised by children's rights campaigners for the punitive approach to addressing the needs of the wider community over the needs of, often very vulnerable, young people. There is some evidence that they are fairly counterproductive as they are considered a *badge of honour* or *right of passage*, by some young people.

Some types of youth work may be frustrated through their use. For example, any positive gains from work with disaffected young people on the street are likely to be undermined if individuals within the group are barred under the terms of their ASBO from entering the area. It can be particularly challenging for the youth worker to undertake positive or rehabilitative work with seriously disaffected young people.

Section 17

Section 17 places a legal duty on the local authority to:

> *exercise its various functions with due regard to the likely effect of the exercise of those functions on, and the need to do all that it reasonably can to prevent crime and disorder in, its area.*

This means that youth work policy and practice must have regard to the impact on crime and disorder within the area. Most youth workers employed by the local authority will automatically fall within the provision; however, even voluntary youth work agencies which depend on local authority grants for funding to run diversionary programmes for young people, are likely to come within the ambit of the provision through the contract they have with the local authority to provide the service.

This can cause a dilemma for the youth worker in deciding at what point they are expected to share information with police and other professional colleagues if they suspect that the behaviour of young people they are working with could be considered by others to be antisocial.

Amendments to the Crime and Disorder Act were introduced by the Anti-social Behaviour Act 2003. This widened the range of people who can apply for ASBOs to include registered social landlords and British Transport Police. It changed the definition of 'public assembly' in the Public Order Act 1986, so that only two people instead of 20 can be assembled within the meaning of the Act. Police and community support officers can issue dispersal orders from a designated area to any group of two or more people. Failure to comply with a dispersal order results in a criminal offence being committed.

Young people have reported that this has caused the greatest detrimental impact on their personal safety and places them at greater risk of becoming the victim of a crime, when they become isolated from their friends. The dispersal order has to be from a designated place and there are particular rules governing the designation of the area.

Police also have discretionary power (Section 30) to return young people under the age of 16 to their home after 9 p.m. The Court of Appeal in *PW, R v. Commissioner of Police of the Metropolis* (2006) has ruled that reasonable force can be used to remove young people to their home. This should not be confused with a curfew order which might be in place, as there are rules to prevent the arbitrary use of these powers. There needs to be, for example, concern for the safety of the young person, and the police will need to take account of their age, circumstances and the time.

The Act created on-the-spot fines for truancy, noise and graffiti and, along with the Police and Justice Act 2005 and the Education and Inspections Act 2006, extended the range of applicants and the criteria for applying for parenting orders.

ACTIVITY **6.2**

Do you think the function of youth work is mainly to divert young people from crime or to secure more effective inclusion of young people in the crime and disorder reduction plans for their area?

What skills do you think the professional youth worker will need to employ in order to be effective in this area of work?

Government policy initially focused on enforcement and punitive measures to reduce anti-social behaviour, but recommendations emanating from *Every Child Matters* and *Youth Matters* suggest that a better balance needs to be sought between engaging young people as active citizens by providing better levels of support during the difficult transition into adulthood, and ensuring communities are safe and cohesive for people of all ages. You might believe that in some areas we have some way to go in striking the right balance between protection of young people's wellbeing and protection of their freedom of movement, a freedom which you will remember is guaranteed under Article 11 of the ECHR.

Youth workers are highly likely to feature as a group of key professionals who are considered to have the skills to undertake specific aspects of the work on prevention of crime, whether that is outreach work with young people who congregate in public places, in order to provide diversionary activities, or finding new ways to engage with and empower young people in a world that is increasingly focused on crime and disorder. One way in which you can be better equipped to empower young people is through an understanding of the scope of the law on antisocial behaviour. Coupled with your knowledge of human rights law and your professional skills in engaging with and empowering young people (discussed in more detail in the following chapter), the role of the professional youth worker is entering a new era with considerable scope for the worker to be fairly creative in their work with vulnerable young people.

The work of the Youth Offending Service

The Youth Offending Service (YOS) was originally established as a multi-agency Youth Offending Team (YOT) in each local authority area, with responsibility for management of young offenders. With key roles in not only reducing re-offending but in preventing offending, the teams commonly comprise social workers, probation officers, police officers, health and youth workers. The YOS prepares plans outlining what they have achieved and what they will achieve in relation to youth offending targets. The YOS reports to the Youth Justice Board.

Youth workers are increasingly choosing to work on this agenda either through the YOS for their area or undertaking direct work with young people on the streets, many of whom are at risk of social exclusion and of becoming victims of crime. There is, arguably, a greater emphasis on taking a more balanced approach to tackling youth offending as we near the end of the decade.

The Youth Crime Action Plan is a comprehensive, cross-government description of what the government is going to do to tackle youth crime. The website describes this as:

> a 'triple track' approach of enforcement and punishment where behaviour is unaccept-able, non-negotiable support and challenge where it is most needed, and better and earlier prevention.

> It makes clear that the government will not tolerate behaviour that causes misery and suffering for innocent victims who more often than not are other young people. People have a responsibility to obey the law if we are to deliver fairness and prosperity to all communities.

In part the Youth Crime Action Plan is a response to the high number of young people in some UK cities who are victims of knife crime and to those who are at risk of becoming involved in gangs. There is an expectation that the youth worker will, alongside the police and in some circumstances with former gang members, proactively work with those young men and women who are gang members or are vulnerable to being involved in gangs.

It is also accepted that although the numbers are relatively small, there is a significant number of young people who live within families where there are complex problems and more innovative solutions need to be taken to address the multiple risk factors some young people are exposed to.

At a national level the government's RESPECT programme has moved from the Home Office to the Department for Children, Schools and Families (DCSF). Popular with housing providers and police alike, RESPECT became well known for its focus on tough, non-negotiable intervention in the lives of young people causing disruption at school or roaming the streets. It distanced itself from what it saw as a soft approach to dealing with young people in difficulty, advocating tough action to reduce nuisance and antisocial behaviour.

When young people have committed crimes

So far we have looked at the situation when young people may be accused of and found to have behaved in an antisocial manner, so this section is focused on young people who have offended.

When a young person is arrested by the police, they should normally be interviewed in the presence of an appropriate adult. This is often their parent but this function might be provided by the YOS. The role of the appropriate adult was established by the Police and Criminal Evidence Act (PACE) 1984, a law that was introduced to provide a greater degree of rigour to the process of arresting, questioning and charging individuals.

When a young person has been arrested the provisions of PACE control the amount of time they can be held and ensure they have access to a solicitor if they ask for it. If the young person attends a police station voluntarily, they are free to leave, unless and until they are placed under arrest.

The role of the appropriate adult is not to replace the legal advice to which the young person is entitled. It is to ensure the young person understands the nature of the allegations against them. The role requirements are set out in Section 66 of PACE (amended by the Serious Organised Crime and Police Act 2005) so it is not proposed to go into them in any great detail here. Training is provided for those who are likely to take on this role in their professional capacity.

If the offence is considered quite minor, the young person may be released. They might, of course, be given a reprimand or referred to the YOS. Another option, particularly if the offence is more serious or is part of a pattern of offending, is to bail the young person to appear in court. There will generally be an assumption in favour of bail rather than accommodating the young person. Only if they are at risk of further offending, are likely to pose a threat to themselves or others, or have previously breached bail conditions, are young people likely to be detained (Section 23 of the Children and Young Person's Act 1969). The grounds for applying for a secure accommodation order are fairly limited and for most offences would not apply. Young people aged 12–16 who are sentenced to custody will have to remain in a secure children's home until the case is heard. These homes are mainly run by the local authority.

For 17 year olds, the only option if the courts refuse bail and insist on detention is to remand the young person in custody. Young offender institutions, which house the majority of young offenders who are over 17, are run by the prison service. A number of enquiries into the deaths of young people on remand have raised the level of concerns over the practice of placing vulnerable young people in custody. The inquests in 2007 into the deaths of a 14 year old and a 15 year old led to an independent review into the use of restraint on young people in detention. The coroner questioned the fitness of the Youth Justice Board in keeping young people safe in custody. You might want to undertake your own research on young offenders in detention as this is outside the scope of this book.

The court processes

One of the outcomes of the European Court ruling into the proceedings in the Bulger case is that the courts must take greater account of the age of young defendants in criminal trials. The proceedings have to be fair and all effort must be made to ensure the young person is able to understand and can, as far as possible, participate in them. They should be able to sit with family members if possible and the usual formalities of dress and wigs worn by the judge should be dispensed with.

Fortin (2006) points to the disparity between the civil law, which expects young people to demonstrate their capacity (for example, in instructing a solicitor), and the criminal law, which presumes children over ten already have the necessary capacity. Fortin questions the appropriateness of subjecting children who commit the most serious crime to the full force of the law. This is in light of successive research which suggests that young people who commit the most serious crimes are often the most emotionally disturbed and least able to understand the seriousness of their crime. Certainly the UK has one of the lowest ages at which young people are deemed competent to stand trial for a crime.

C H A P T E R   R E V I E W

- Young people are more likely to be the victims of crime than they are to be the perpetrators.

- The Youth Crime Action Plan extends the British Crime Survey to under 16s for the first time.

- Research shows that some young people might be at higher risk of offending than others and that the cumulative effect of more than one risk factor increases the likelihood of becoming involved in crime.

- The risks of offending are offset by protective factors such as social and emotional confidence, positive parenting and educational attainment.

- The Crime and Disorder Act 1998 introduced:

  - Crime and Disorder Reduction Partnerships;

  - Antisocial Behaviour Orders (ASBO);

  - Youth Offending Services.

  And abolished:

  - The presumption (*doli incapax*) that children under 14 did not fully understand the full nature or consequences of criminal acts and it was up to the prosecution to show otherwise.

- The Antisocial Behaviour Act 2003:

  - extended the range of people who could apply for parenting orders;

  - allows the police and community support officers to issue dispersal orders to young people in a designated area;

  - creates on-the-spot fines;

  - enables the police to return a young person home using reasonable force after 9 p.m.

FURTHER READING

Youth matters Green Paper 2005. London: The Stationery Office.

Anderson, R, Brown, I, Dowty, T, Inglesant, P, Heath, W and Sasse, A (2009) *Database state*. York: Joseph Rowntree Reform Trust.

Department of Children, Schools and Families (2007) *Aiming high for young people: ten year strategy for positive activities*. London: DCSF.

Echo (2007) *Hoodies or altar boys? What is media stereotyping doing to our British boys?* Women in Journalism, **www.womeninjournalism.co.uk/node/321**

Fortin, J (2003) *Children's rights and the developing law.* London: LexisNexis.

Feinstein, L (2008) *Tired of hanging around – using sport and leisure activities to prevent anti-social behaviour by young people.* London: Audit Commission.

Garner, R (2009) 'Hoodies, louts, scum': how media demonises teenagers. *The Independent,* 13 March.

Morgan, DL (1988) *Focus groups as qualitative research.* London: Sage.

Respect Taskforce (2006) *Respect action plan.* London: The Stationery Office.

Smith, C and Allen, J (2004) *Home Office Report 18/04.* London: Home Office online.

McCabe, A (2006) *National evaluation of the Children's Fund.* University of Birmingham.

WEBSITES

www.nya.org.uk

www.dcsf.gov.uk

www.independent.co.uk

www.everychildmatters.gov.uk/youthmatters/positiveactivities/

www.crimereduction.homeoffice.gov.uk/legislation

www.opsi.gov.uk/acts

www.jrrt.org.uk

REFERENCES

Children and Young Person's Act 1969. London: HMSO.

Police and Criminal Evidence Act 1984. London: HMSO.

Public Order Act 1986. London: HMSO.

Youth crime action plan 1988. London: HMSO.

Crime and Disorder Act 1998. London: The Stationery Office.

Every child matters Green Paper 2003. London: The Stationery Office.

Serious Organised Crime and Police Act 2005. London: The Stationery Office.

Youth matters Green Paper 2005. London: The Stationery Office.

Youth crime action plan 2008. London: The Stationery Office.

Anderson, R, Brown, I, Dowty, T, Inglesant, P, Heath, W and Sasse, A (2009) *Database state.* York: Joseph Rowntree Reform Trust.

Feinstein (2008) *Tired of hanging around – using sport and leisure activities to prevent anti-social behaviour by young people.* London: Audit Commission.

Fortin, J (2006) *Children's rights and the developing law.* London: LexisNexis.

Laming, Lord (2009) *The protection of children in England: a progress report.* London: The Stationery Office.

Lifelong Learning UK (2008*) National occupational standards for youth work.* London: Lifelong Learning UK.

McHugh, R (2008) *How does the reluctant worker work with the reluctant gangster? Interpolate and emancipate or perpetuate?* Leicester: National Youth Association –
www.nya.org.uk/files/120599/FileName/nyapiece.doc

Morgan, DL (1988) *Focus groups as qualitative research.* London: Sage.

Respect Taskforce (2006) *Respect action plan.* London: The Stationery Office.

Smith, C and Allen, J (2004) *Home Office Report 18/04.* London: Home Office online.

CASES

T v. *UK*; *V* v. *UK* (2000) 30 EHRR 121.

PW, R (on the application of) v. *Commissioner of Police for the Metropolis & Anor* [2006] WCA Civ 458 (11 May 2006).

Chapter 7
Participation and freedom of expression

The case for promoting participation

The participation agenda has been gaining momentum in the last decade. This is due in part to an increased recognition that, as the cases for increasing public consultation and user involvement have gained greater credibility at a national level, it is no longer justifiable or ethical to exclude children and young people. You will already notice that within the first paragraph the words participation, consultation, involvement and inclusion are all referred to, yet mean different things. Before we attempt to distinguish their meanings, we will consider why participation is considered important.

There are a number of different reasons for increasing the involvement of young people, and although they are not in any particular priority order they are summarised below:

- *The economic case*: ensuring services better meet the needs of young people and reducing expenditure on services that don't meet their needs.

- *The moral case*: developing young people's self-belief that they are able to have influence on the things that most affect their lives.

- *The legislative case*: giving effect to the provisions of the UNCRC, the Children Act 1989 and the ECHR.

There is increasing acceptance of the need to ensure young people become involved in decision making about public services as this, in turn, ensures that the services are better tailored to meeting their needs collectively and at an individual level. It does not always rest comfortably with politicians, policy makers or practitioners and there is huge variation across the UK in how young people's participation is given practical effect. For example, despite greater levels of participation by the general public in community safety initiatives, there are relatively few examples of young people being successfully included in planning or developing measures to address crime at a local level.

This is partly due to a belief that adults are better placed to make important decisions about the safety and wellbeing of young people. This is particularly true when there is a conflict between an adult and young person's view of what is in the young person's best interest (Chapter 3) and partly because negative images of young people persist and create among professionals a reluctance to include or engage positively with them. You will have seen in the previous chapter that this view is prevalent despite the young person's greater risk of being the victim of a crime.

For most professional youth workers the failure to take measures to actively include young people might seem at odds with your professional values. The National Occupational Standards are explicit about the requirement on youth workers to *promote young people's self awareness, confidence and participation* (1.3) and *work with young people in promoting their rights* (2.1).

ACTIVITY 7.1

Imagine you are asked by your employer to develop a participation strategy for young people. How would you approach this task? What key features might the strategy include? Make a note of these before reading on.

For the purpose of this exercise a strategy can be defined as: *the means by which objectives are achieved over the longer term*. Your participation strategy should therefore begin with a statement of these objectives. This is important for a number of reasons but primarily because young people are likely to want to know why they are being asked to participate, what they are being invited to participate in, and what difference their involvement will make. Being clear about the objectives at the outset enables progress to be measured against them.

You are unlikely to undertake this task alone so it is important that those you are working with share a vision of what is going to be achieved through a participation strategy, otherwise you are unlikely to get very far. You will probably want to give careful consideration to the point at which young people themselves will be involved and what techniques you will use to make their involvement meaningful. It should be a valuable learning process rather than a dull writing by committee exercise.

If you are working for a local authority, you might also want to get the support of elected members of the council. Each local authority has a named local councillor with lead responsibility for children and young people (Children Act 2004). This elected member could be a useful advocate in publicising the strategy. Their involvement will also give young people an opportunity to take part in the democratic process, as most of the young people you are likely to be working with are below voting age and their opportunities for engaging with politicians is fairly limited.

Another consideration (covered in the next chapter) is how the most commonly excluded young people – those with disabilities or poor health, those who are homeless or living in temporary accommodation, or those from minority ethnic or faith groups – are empowered to be part of the process.

The meaning of participation

How should we define participation? The National Youth Agency (NYA) defines it as *the active involvement of children and young people.* This would appear to distinguish participation from those activities where young people are routinely consulted and either their recommendations are ignored or they are implemented only in part. It is, therefore, more than just consultation. Participation is further defined by the NYA as the *process by which children and young people influence decision making which brings about change in them, others, their service and their communities.*

A number of initiatives with the aim of expanding young people's participation are under way. *Participation Works* is an online gateway hub for sharing information, ideas and progress towards more effective participation. Among a number of proposals designed to give young people a greater say in how local services are run, a consortia of children's charities has been selected to develop the *Young Inspectors* programme. This programme will run for two years from 2009 and enable teams of up to 30 young people aged 13–19 to operate in 36 areas, influencing local policy and planning of services.

Many other current government policies exist, such as the funding provided by the government through the Youth Media Fund to enable young people to *take part in media projects using print, television, film, radio, digital or online media to express their views on issues that matter to them.*

The DCSF website describes the aims of MediaBox as helping young people:

> *gain transferable skills and experience to better prepare them for entering adulthood and the world of work. The fund is targeted at young people from disadvantaged backgrounds who are most at risk of not achieving the five* Every Child Matters *outcomes. The fund aims to empower young people to take responsibility to develop activities to make a difference in their local communities and to benefit local people. By producing projects that reflect young people's views and aspirations the fund also aims to influence policymakers by providing them with young people's perspectives on issues that affect their daily lives. MediaBox also aims to improve the portrayal of young people in the media and provide employers including the media industry with trainees from backgrounds and with experiences under-represented in the workforce.*

Article 12 of the UNCRC states that:

1 *States Parties shall assure to the child who is capable of forming his or her own views the right to express those views freely in all matters affecting the child, the views of the child being given due weight in accordance with the age and maturity of the child.*

2 *For this purpose, the child shall in particular be provided the opportunity to be heard in any judicial and administrative proceedings affecting the child, either directly, or through a representative or an appropriate body, in a manner consistent with the procedural rules of national law.*

Article 13 gives the young person the right to freedom of expression provided they respect others and Article 17 enables young people to receive, seek and provide information.

The establishment of a Children's Commissioner for each of the UK countries with a role in promoting awareness of young people's views and interests goes some considerable way forward from previous government measures to promote young people's inclusion in decision making.

Specific domestic legislation, including the Children Act 1989 which requires social workers to consider the wishes and feelings of young people in family law proceedings, is not generally applicable to all children. Similarly, changes in legislation to ensure consultation with young people who are the subjects of child protection or child in need assessments created by the Children Act 2004 are limited to a relatively small number of young people, as is the obligation to promote the participation in public life of disabled people (Disability Discrimination Act 2005).

Although it is highly laudable that efforts are being made by legislators to incorporate the views, wishes and interests of young people, it could be argued that the law is complex in respect of young people's routine inclusion in decision making about the things that matter most to them. Youth workers might want to question how far the law goes to ensure young people are routinely asked for their opinion on a wide range of topics that affect their daily lives. The wording in the UNCRC is, after all, giving due weight to the child *in accordance with the age and maturity of the child.*

How far will participative approaches, however well intended, address the needs of young people who are most likely to be excluded because of their presumed level of maturity or their capacity to express their views in a manner which is acceptable to those in authority?

Many of the activities designed to promote participation might be extremely effective at helping young people to mobilise in order to present a collective view on matters of policy and practice, but do they go far enough to help individual young people to express their views on matters that concern them?

Purpose of participation

The first reason given for increasing participation is an economic one: the idea that by including young people in their design, services can be better tailored to provide what is needed rather than what is presumed to be needed. Certainly the thrust of successive government policies has been to design services that are more effective at producing better outcomes rather than merely focused on increasing output. This is a considerable shift away from the ethos of doing more of the same thing in the hope that young people will participate in greater numbers, and towards a more sophisticated analysis of what can achieve the best result.

It makes good sense to gain a better understanding from young people of what their needs are, and there are many examples of good practice but the concrete research available on the actual cost benefit of involving young people is not yet fully established.

A report compiled by Ken Warpole in 2003, for the environmental group Groundwork makes a compelling argument for including young people in the design of urban open spaces, which comes close to providing the economic argument for inclusion. Presented through a series of case studies conducted in the UK and in Northern Europe, the report provides evidence for moving away from the purchase of standardised play equipment and towards more imaginative use of open space that caters for young people of all ages. When young people are included in decision making about the design and use of the public realm, their investment of time and skills is rewarded by better used and better cared for open spaces than those from which they had been excluded. When young people do not participate, often as a consequence of risk adverse planning processes and poor participation strategies, play areas catering almost exclusively for very young children tend to dominate the landscape. With 81 per cent of 15–19 year olds expressing dissatisfaction with the quality of outdoor spaces where they could meet to socialise with friends, there would seem to be a strong economic case for increasing the proportion of young people who participate in public space planning. The indirect costs to young people's physical health and emotional wellbeing of spending too little time outdoors or being limited to using poorly designed outdoor environments are fairly well documented.

The moral reasons for increasing young people's participation are similarly compelling. There is steadily increasing recognition that young people have their own unique perspective on the world and that if we are expecting their development as complete human beings by the time they reach adulthood, we should provide opportunities for them to learn through making decisions and taking some responsibility for them.

Our views on childhood have changed enormously over the last 20 years. Once seen only as a part of their family or, if they lived in public care, as part of a group of looked after children, their views were rarely taken into account. The impact of excluding young people has been detrimental, with reported increases in mental ill health and depression among young people, increases in risky behaviour and coping strategies which have a negative impact on how they are viewed by others and on their aspirations for the future.

Youth work as a profession has often led the way in campaigning for young people to be recognised and valued for their own contribution. We have, arguably, some way to go before this view is universally accepted.

Fortin (2003) cites the relatively backward stance taken in the UK to the promotion of young people's rights to participate within the school setting. The law excludes children from becoming school governors, although since 2003 they are able to become associate members of school governing bodies, and, therefore, it falls short of a specific legal duty to consult with pupils over school policy. Although many schools within the UK have set up school councils, their role in the administration of the school can be fairly piecemeal and limited to a very small number of pupils. This is despite evidence that when young people are included in a more systematic way in developing responsible behaviour policies, there are reported improvements in behaviour among all pupils. The Education Act 2005 provides that account be given (Section 7) to the views of stakeholders, including students, when undertaking inspections.

In 'Children's human rights as a force for change', Willow (2005) advocates the creation of a human rights framework to increase participation among children and young people. Pointing to the fact that a significant proportion of the population is unable to participate in democracy because they can't vote despite calls from human rights groups to reduce the age at which young people can vote to 16, there is widespread reluctance to extend this right. As young people can lawfully engage in sexual activity and can be treated as adults in decision making about health care, why not then have a say in how public services are run? At the beginning of the twenty-first century do we not have to be more creative about the means we use as professionals to equip young people with the skills to participate effectively?

Levels of participation

Hart (1997) produced what has become known as the ladder of youth participation. Each rung on the ladder represents how young people are incorporated into decision making. At the top of the ladder, on the eighth rung, young people and adults share decision making and all the responsibilities that this entails. The bottom three rungs are, Hart

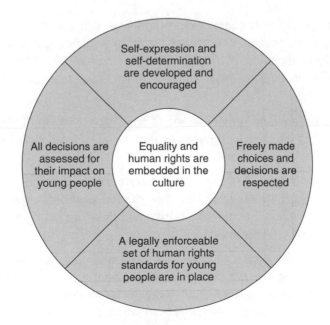

Figure 7.1 Embedding freedom of expression

argues, tokenistic, as children and young people may be present but are not meaningfully included. Rungs four to seven represent varying degrees of involving young people. Although the ladder is widely used, it is submitted that the utopian view of young people who are equal decision makers at the top of the ladder gives the impression that activities at lower rungs of the ladder are somewhat inferior. Figure 7.1 is proposed as an alternative model for considering participation as a part of what is a fundamental human right to freedom of expression.

Freedom of expression

Freedom of expression is fundamental to young people's full and equal inclusion as human beings deserving of rights. It is, after all, through freedom of expression that people are able to give visible (and audible) effect to their freedom of conscience.

In the United States the protection is given in law to free speech, which means that other forms of self-expression do not have the same level of protection. The interpretation by the courts of the extent to which free speech is guaranteed has received some publicity over what type of material can be publicised on the internet. This has led to a generous interpretation of the constitutional right, even when the effect is to pose risks to others. The publication of the names and addresses of doctors who undertake lawful abortions has led to the murder of a number of doctors and this has caused considerable disquiet over how far free speech should be protected when it interferes with the human rights of others.

By contrast, the scope of the provision contained in Article 10 of the ECHR is much wider insofar as it covers a much wider range of expression including art, film and broadcasting. It therefore protects young people's rights to protest using a variety of means.

Article 10 states that:

> *Everyone has the right to freedom of expression. This right shall include freedom to hold opinions and to receive and impart information and ideas without interference by public authority and regardless of frontiers. This Article shall not prevent States from requiring the licensing of broadcasting, television or cinema enterprises.*

The courts have, however, been more willing to limit the expression of this right when it has been deemed to interfere with public health, morality, freedoms of others and the prevention of crime and public order.

Much of the current debate on young people's human rights centres on the provisions of the UNCRC, but you will remember from the chapter on human rights that the UN Convention, albeit monitored by the commission and therefore having significant persuasive effect, is not legally enforceable.

The HRA 1998 gives direct effect to the ECHR. Although it was not designed specifically with them in mind, it nevertheless applies equally to young people. It is undoubtedly an indication of the relative powerlessness of young people in society that few challenges to young people's right to free expression have been before the courts.

CASE STUDY

Hardeep is a 14-year-old Sikh boy. He decides to wear brightly coloured turbans to school instead of the more discreet keski *which he had worn beforehand. The head of year has asked him to refrain from wearing such bright colours as they are not in keeping with the school uniform policy and has told him not to return to school until he resumes wearing his* keski *once more.*

What rights does Hardeep have to self-expression in the school environment?

Can he be excluded from school for refusing to conform to the uniform policy?

The right of young people to wear particular types of clothing and jewellery in order to freely express their beliefs has received considerable prominence in the last few years. A case that hit international headlines in 2007 concerned the exclusion from a school in France of three Sikh boys on the grounds of their refusal to remove their turbans. In June 2008 their case was lodged with the European Court of Human Rights on the grounds that a law introduced in France in 2004 which prohibits all visible displays of faith in secular schools was a breach of the ECHR.

In the Court of Appeal in March 2005, a young Muslim woman won the right to wear full traditional dress in the classroom, arguing successfully that the school had:

• unlawfully excluded her;

• denied her the right to manifest her religion; and

• denied her access to suitable and appropriate education.

However, in 2007, a 12-year-old Muslim schoolgirl lost her legal battle to wear the *niqab* (covering her whole face) while she is being taught by male teachers.

In 2007 a young woman was asked to remove a purity ring which she wore as a symbol of her intention to refrain from pre-marital sexual activity on religious grounds. She cited the ECHR, but her case was ultimately dismissed as the court held that the ring was not a recognised symbol of Christianity and the school was within its rights to ban it as part of their 'no jewellery' policy.

The 1983 case of *Mandla* v. *Lee* which came before the House of Lords confirmed that Sikhs could be defined as a race, not just a religious group, and therefore fell within the scope of the protection offered by the Race Relations Act 1976.

ACTIVITY 7.2

Do you think that state schools should be able to require pupils to dress in specific ways? Would your answer differ if pupils were citing cultural rather than religious reasons for deviating from the school uniform?

In November 2008 results of a survey undertaken by the charity Beatbullying showed that one in four children with a religious belief are bullied for that belief. This has led to calls for improvements to recording and monitoring of faith-based bullying in schools similar to that employed to address racist and homophobic bullying.

The scope of freedom of expression

Not only does Article 10 allow freedom of expression, it may be an important tool for gaining access to information. The right to impart information is, after all, of limited use if there is no corresponding right for others to receive that information. A 1992 case against Ireland concerned the production of information by Dublin Well Women clinic on abortion services available in England, despite the prohibition on abortion in Ireland. The European Court held that Ireland had acted unlawfully in attempting to prevent women from receiving information on medical treatments available in other countries.

In the UK the decision to hold the inquiry into the death of a large number of elderly patients at the hands of GP Harold Shipman was held by the Divisional Court to be in the public interest and, therefore, it was decided that it should be a public inquiry. These examples should give you some idea of the role the court will play in balancing the rights of different parties, including their rights to privacy, when deciding whether or not a violation of Article 10 has occurred. There does appear to be a common public interest thread running through these cases.

As a youth worker, you are likely to be asked to take part in integrated planning in respect of the young people you are working with and may face some conflict over whether information you are given in confidence about a young person should remain so or whether the young person has a right to that information. The purpose of part 2 of Article 10 is to strike a balance between the scope of freedom of expression and the wider interest of society and the protection of others. The limitations on the freedom of expression must also be necessary in a democratic society and the courts have taken a fairly robust approach to upholding democratic principles.

The scope of the freedom does not automatically protect all rights of access to information but there are other laws that significantly extend these rights. For example, there are greater rights to access information that is of general public interest through the Freedom of Information Act 2000 and to gain access to personal information held about you through the Data Protection Act 1998.

Right to self-determination in court

The rights of young people to participate fully in proceedings that have a bearing on their lives is dependent to a large extent on how flexibly the courts interpret the provision in the Children Act to *have regard to the ascertainable wishes and feelings of the child*. Eekelaar (2002) argues that this is sometimes outweighed by the indeterminacy of the welfare principle, which can allow the judge to take into account almost any factor and determine its relevance to the case. It is not always clear whether the judge is taking a long-term or a short-term view when weighing the young person's view against other welfare considerations. There is also the risk of substituting the adult views of what is in a young person's interests rather than allowing young people to determine what is in their own best interests.

It makes it difficult, therefore, to see how the HRA has helped to progress a young person's right to self-determination within the court arena. The issue of age and maturity of the young person is complex, and research shows that much depends on the context in which the decision is being made. The judiciary seem happy, however, to accept that the vast majority of adolescents are capable of expressing a view and of having this view accepted. The exceptions tend to be where the risk is high, for example, in the issue of medical treatment where the risk is of death, although the courts in 2008 upheld a competent 13 year old's right to refrain from further invasive treatment that might have prolonged her life in favour of allowing her to die with dignity. Again the context is important and the courts will take a range of factors into account.

Some anomalies persist, such as the decision in *Re B* (change of surname) which prevented the children from formally taking the name of their stepfather, despite their ages (16, 14 and 12). The judge did accept that they could informally use whatever name they chose, but this approach might have seemed to them to fly in the face of their right to make reasonable choices about their future.

The courts are similarly alert to potential indoctrination which they recognise comes in many forms and have intervened to override decisions about medical treatment and about contact with an absent parent despite the young person's objections. The courts have, however, been criticised over giving contact rights in the face of allegations of domestic abuse where young person has indicated that they do not want to have contact with the abusive parent.

CASE STUDY

In 2006, 12-year-old Molly Campbell sparked a nationwide search when she went missing from her family home. Within a few days it became clear that she had left Scotland in the company of her older sister and had flown to Lahore to be with her father.

She signed a statement to say she had freely chosen to remain in Pakistan and wanted to be raised in the Muslim faith. She expressed unwillingness to return to the care of her mother and stepfather and wished to be known by her new name Misbah Iram Ahmed Rana.

One of the biggest challenges you will face as a professional working with young people is the fine line that will exist between young people's own right to make decisions about their lives and the potential consequences of these.

Your role in engaging with, and building trusted relationships with, young people will inevitably lead you to question your own values and beliefs. You are not expected to understand the full scope of the law as it applies to young people's freedom of expression. The law is constantly changing and evolving through new legislation, and new interpretation by the courts of existing legislation. You will hopefully develop an interest in keeping abreast of these developments as they are widely reported in the national press as well as in professional youth work publications, and use these examples to encourage an honest dialogue with young people, so that they continue to develop the skills to make their own decisions and their right to make mistakes.

CHAPTER REVIEW

- Changes in the law and in government policy over the last ten years have led to an increased awareness of the relevance of promoting young people's participation in public life.

- Youth work is a key element in the work to increase young people's right to self-determination and their greater visibility in public debate.

- There are specific requirements in the National Occupational Standards for Youth Work which make the promotion of the participative agenda part of your continuing professional development as practitioners.

- Freedom of expression is a fundamental principle on which effective participation is based and is a legally enforceable right.

- A number of different legal rules apply to young people's right to receive and give information.

- The right to self-determination includes the right to make mistakes and learn from them.

FURTHER READING

Eekelaar, J (2002) Beyond the welfare principle. *Child and Family Law Quarterly*, 14: 237.

Fortin, J (2003) *Children's rights and the developing law.* London: LexisNexis.

Warpole, K (2003) *No particular place to go: children, young people and public space.* Birmingham: Groundwork Trust.

WEBSITES

www.dcsf.gov.uk

www.groundwork.org.uk

www.independent.co.uk

www.beatbullying.org

www.nyas.org

www.participationworks.org.uk/

www.freechild.org/ladder.htm

REFERENCES

Race Relations Act 1976. London: The Stationery Office.

Children Act 1989. London: The Stationery Office.

Data Protection Act 1998. London: The Stationery Office.

Human Rights Act 1998. London: The Stationery Office.

Freedom of Information Act 2000. London: The Stationery Office.

Children Act 2004. London: The Stationery Office.

Disability Discrimination Act 2005. London: The Stationery Office.

Education Act 2005. London: The Stationery Office.

Council of Europe (2002) *Convention for the protection of human rights and fundamental freedoms.* Strasbourg: Council of Europe.

Eekelaar, J (2002) Beyond the welfare principle. *Child and Family Law Quarterly,* 14: 237.

Fortin, J (2003) *Children's rights and the developing law.* London: LexisNexis.

Hart, R (1997) *Children's participation: the theory and practice of involving young citizens in community development and environmental care.* London: Earthscan Publications.

Lifelong Learning UK (2008) *National occupational standards for youth work.* London: Lifelong Learning UK.

United Nations (1989) *Convention on the rights of the child.* New York: Office of the United Nations High Commissioner for Human Rights.

Warpole, K (2003) *No particular place to go: children, young people and public space.* Birmingham: Groundwork Trust.

Willow, C (2005) Children's human rights as a force for change, in Harvey, C (ed) *Human rights in the community: rights as agents for change.* Oxford: Hart.

CASES

Mandla v. *Lee* 1983

re B (Children) (FC). [2008] UKHL 35.

Chapter 8
Developing inclusive practice

C H A P T E R   O B J E C T I V E S

By the end of this chapter you should have:

- a better understanding of what constitutes effective youth work practice and how to meet the required professional occupational standards, particularly those which:

  - facilitate learning and development of young people (1.1);

  - promote equality and value diversity (2.3);

  - facilitate change (4.3);

  - develop colleagues (5.3).

- clearer ideas about how you as a professional worker should respond to the immediate needs of young people and contribute to their successful transition into adulthood;

- explored the obligations the professional youth worker has in promoting the rights of the most marginalised and commonly excluded young people;

- embarked on the first stage of your journey of continuous professional development.

This chapter brings together some of the themes discussed in previous chapters and considers the wider issue of your professional competence. You have had a chance to explore some of your legal obligations through the various exercises contained in this book and have, hopefully, taken the opportunity to use them as discussion points with your professional colleagues. This chapter is more about your professional development and how this is regulated through a set of standards that apply to your work as well as by the legal principles outlined in this book and elsewhere.

You will have noticed that throughout the book reference is made to youth work as a profession, but what exactly do we mean by this? Is it possible to be a youth worker who is unprofessional? The reason for the distinction is that until relatively recently there were myriad different qualifications that led to a professional youth work qualification. This led to confusion about what employers could expect from youth workers and what standard the youth worker needed to operate at. There was considerable variation across England as well as between youth work practice in Scotland, Wales and Northern Ireland.

Professional youth work status is acquired through a higher educational study route leading to one of the following nationally recognised qualifications:

- a Diploma in Higher Education (Dip HE);

- a BA (Hons) degree;

- a postgraduate certificate and (MA) Masters degree.

There are a number of universities and colleges of higher education that offer these qualifications through both full-time and part-time study combined with the successful completion of practice placements. More detailed information is available through the NYA which regulates the pre-professional youth work routes.

Pre-professional status of youth support worker is achieved through the National Vocational Qualifications (NVQs) and Vocationally Related Qualifications (VRQs) routes.

From September 2010 there is a requirement that all new youth work qualifications must be at degree level or higher. Youth work qualifications acquired before this date will still confer qualified youth worker status, as the change will not be implemented retrospectively.

The rationale for regulating the children and young people's workforce has emanated from successive inquiries into systemic failures in professional practice which have led to inadequate protection of those who are most at risk. This, coupled with the widely held perception that young people and those working with them should have higher aspirations, has led to the changes in government policy on the regulation and development of the children and young people's workforce.

There is a broad recognition that if we are to implement the recommendations from public inquiries such as those led by Laming (2003; 2009) and ensure that all those working with young people conform to a high standard of professional competence, an overhaul of the qualification system itself is inevitable.

In summary, these reforms affect the professional youth worker in three specific ways:

- revision of the professional qualification;

- adoption of a set of common standards of practice; and

- enhanced checks with the Criminal Records Bureau of all those who have access to young people.

ACTIVITY *8.1*

Imagine you are asked to demonstrate your capabilities as a youth worker to potential employers. Young people and community representatives will form part of the recruitment and selection team.

- *What criteria might a young person use to judge a youth worker's abilities?*

- *What would a parent or member of the community expect of a professional youth worker?*

ACTIVITY **8.1** *continued*

- *How might you distinguish youth work from other professional disciplines?*

- *What do you think an employer should expect from a professional youth worker?*

Make a list under each heading.

Did you have different criteria listed against each group or did you find that your lists were fairly consistent? You might have found that some things appeared to conflict with others.

You may have begun with a set of values that distinguishes youth work from other types of intervention in young people's lives and included securing a young person's voluntary engagement. This would appear to be a fundamental principle of effective youth work practice which begins with the premise that young people's views of the world should be respected and that they can choose whether or not to engage.

Ironically this is an aspect of youth work that other professions often find most challenging. The youth work role in developing young people's skills and attitudes, rather than remedying perceived and actual problems with behaviour or achievement through their intervention, can pose some difficulties in multidisciplinary work. A fuller statement of principles and values in youth work can be found in *Ethical Conduct in Youth Work* (nya.org.uk).

You might find that a community member or another professional is likely to want you to undertake duties that seem to contradict what a young person expects of you.

You do not have to meet all of these but you have probably already realised that, in addition to valuing young people, being a positive role model and being consistent yet flexible is part of your role. If you are able to do this and manage other people's expectations of your competence to perform your role effectively, you are doing what is expected of you as a skilled professional youth worker.

Throughout your professional studies you will be asked to provide evidence of your learning. It will form a key part of the assessment of your competence to practise.

As well as having a recognised professional qualification, you should expect to be managed in a way that allows you to demonstrate how you remain competent to undertake a wide variety of roles and aptitudes.

You should be able to demonstrate good interpersonal skills and show how you build effective relationships with young people as well as with other professionals. The National Occupational Standards sets out the framework for you to demonstrate your abilities. You can expect your ability to lead and inspire others, to demonstrate your commitment to promoting equality, to valuing diversity and to challenging oppressive practices to be measured through workplace performance appraisals.

Youth work is now recognised as part of an armoury of interventions that form part of the local offer to young people as part of the ten-year strategy for positive activities which are aimed at improving the life chances of all young people. Contained within *Aiming high for young people* the initiatives come under three main headings:

- *empowerment*: giving young people and communities real influence;

- *access*: attracting and engaging every young person;

- *quality*: effective services delivered by a skilled workforce.

In addition to the improvement of facilities for young people and the degree of influence young people have over them there are key recommendations on developing the youth workforce.

Since the publication at the end of 2007 of *The Children's Plan*, which set out the government's vision for developing integrated services for children, young people and their families, the focus for the professional youth worker is on the provision of integrated youth support. Services are expected to offer a broad and balanced range of activities open to all young people, within which those who are experiencing difficulties will be offered services tailored to their specific needs.

There is a particular emphasis on setting clear goals on involving and including young people in a local authority area in positive activities, on the investment in improved facilities for young people, on clear and accessible information and advice services, and on the provision of specialist support for young people from particular groups to help address the difficulties they face.

ACTIVITY *8.2*

Which groups of young people might need more specialist support? What are the main reasons for targeting additional resources at some groups of young people?

Make a list of the groups of young people who might benefit from additional support.

Youth work has a long tradition of working with marginalised and socially excluded groups of young people; those where adverse family, housing or community factors place them at higher risk of disadvantage.

Some of these were discussed under risk factors in Chapter 6, although it is also recognised that a much wider range of young people who face particular disadvantages will need some additional support.

There are a large number of examples of professional and informal quasi-professional work with young people who are leaving care, young women, or work with lesbian, gay and bisexual young people. Youth workers have achieved recognition in developing international and cross-community work, bringing together groups from different communities as well as specific work with black and minority ethnic young people and young people from different backgrounds on joint projects.

With the current focus on the development of integrated youth support youth workers are increasingly likely to work in locality-based teams bringing together staff from a range of disciplines and with different values. Professional youth workers have, however, a good track record at working in partnership with other agencies and engaging with different professionals. There are examples of youth work in schools where the worker works alongside teachers and school health professionals providing advice and support to young people on aspects of physical, sexual and mental health. Youth workers have worked within housing services with homeless young people, alongside social workers, youth justice workers and the police. The alliance has not always been an easy one but there are good examples of effective multi-agency work where the distinctive contribution of each profession is recognised and utilised.

Youth work has played a part in engaging with the most isolated and at risk young people through the development of the Connexions service, set up to provide information, advice and careers guidance to young people aged 13 to 19.

The reason for the change in policy given by the DCSF in *Aiming High* is:

> high quality youth work, delivered by third and statutory sectors, is central to delivering our ambition of increasing the number of young people on the path to success and an important function of integrated youth support services.

(HM Treasury/DCSF 2007)

The policy document *Every Child Matters: change for children* sets out the context for the improvement in the wellbeing of children and young people from birth to 19. It aims for every child and young person, whatever their background or circumstances, to have the support they need to:

- be healthy;
- stay safe;
- enjoy and achieve;
- make a positive contribution;
- achieve economic wellbeing.

These five 'ECM outcomes' underpin all aspects of government policy relating to children and young people. Policy specifically relating to young people was set out in *Youth Matters* (2005), and *Youth Matters: next steps* (2006), which developed proposals for a *radical reshaping of universal services for teenagers – with targeted support for those who need it most*.

The Education and Inspections Act 2006 (Section 6) created a statutory duty on local authorities, working in partnership with the voluntary and private sectors, to promote the wellbeing of young people aged 13 to 19 (up to 25 for those with learning difficulties) through securing access to educational and positive recreational activities. This gives effect to the proposals contained in *Youth Matters* which set out minimum requirements for young people to have access to:

- sports, including formal and informal team sports and other activities such as outdoor adventure, aerobics and dance;
- constructive activities in clubs, youth groups and classes, young people's own hobbies and interests; personal, social and spiritual development activities; study support; activities encouraging creativity, innovation and enterprise; and residential opportunities;

- opportunities to volunteer, campaign and fundraise;

- safe and enjoyable places to spend time, including socialising with friends.

The responsibility for promoting positive outcomes for young people is a shared responsibility and while youth work as a profession is undergoing major transformation it is within the broader context of the wider improvements in the children and young people's workforce. The assessment of whether or not the young people's workforce actually meets the challenges ahead comes within the ambit of the external inspection regime which reviews local authorities' capacity to deliver, as well as their capacity to continuously improve.

In Chapter 1 we looked at the wider range of professional competencies that underpin youth work and, although you can expect to receive feedback and support for your learning during the qualifying stage of your career, the responsibility for your continued professional development ultimately lies with you. It is no longer acceptable to adopt a laissez-faire attitude to young people's wellbeing, achievement and social inclusion.

Promoting inclusive and anti-oppressive practice

At the beginning of the chapter we discussed the requirements for youth workers to meet fairly generic competencies that are relevant for their work with all young people, but there are specific responsibilities the professional youth worker has to challenge discrimination and to include those young people who are most commonly excluded.

Referred to variously as 'hard to reach' or 'hard to engage', there are many young people who find it difficult to access provision that other young people take for granted. Despite an increasing range of activities for young people, there is evidence of discrimination against some sections of the community. Discrimination not only increases the risk of harm from violent acts against some young people, it causes anxiety, insecurity and fear among whole communities. Discrimination is morally indefensible as well as being unlawful.

Effective youth work can be a powerful way to bring communities together to explore their diversity and learn about each other. It is the responsibility of those who design and provide services to ensure they are accessible to all young people and not the responsibility of those isolated young people to find ways to navigate inaccessible services.

The law has sought for some time to outlaw certain types of discrimination through different pieces of legislation such as the Race Relations Act 1976, the Sex Discrimination Act 1975 and the Disability Discrimination Act 1995.

Subsequent laws such as the Sexual Offences Amendment Act 2000 formally equalised the age of consent for sexual activity. The 2005 Disability Discrimination Act extended the scope of previous legislation to include people and circumstances that were outside the ambit of prior legislative provision.

One of the most significant pieces of legislation is undoubtedly the Race Relations (Amendment) Act 2000 which places a duty on public authorities to undertake impact assessments on all their policies and practices. This law was enacted as a direct response to the report, in 1999, by Sir William Macpherson of an inquiry into the circumstances surrounding the racially motivated murder of teenager Stephen Lawrence. The report criticised the Metropolitan Police Service for their failure to conduct a proper investigation, hampered by what has become widely known as 'institutional racism'. The inquiry found that the negative assumptions about individuals founded on their race, faith or ethnic origin were the primary cause of the failure by the police to properly investigate the murder and bring the perpetrators to justice. It is this that the 2000 Act attempts to address. Similar impact assessments will be required to address other types of discrimination.

CASE STUDY

On the way home from the youth club a group of young people target two young Asian men whom they subject to a torrent of verbal abuse. The young men are jostled and one of them is pushed against a wall. Although neither victim is physically injured, they are frightened by the incident and fearful of reporting it.

The young people who have perpetrated the assault are overheard by the youth worker bragging about the incident and offering to post the video they have made of the incident onto the internet.

The important thing to note is that although there are no visible or recorded injuries, both the harassment and the fear of physical injury are criminal offences. The Offences Against the Person Act (OAPA) 1861 covers both the battery (the physical contact) and the assault (Section 42). An assault is defined as: *any act by which a person intentionally or recklessly causes another person to apprehend immediate and unlawful and personal violence*. In reality it is used only when there is no actual physical harm (Section 47). However, the Crime and Disorder Act 1998 takes the criminal law much further as crimes which have a racial motivation are classified as having an aggravating factor. If the prosecution can show that the offence was motivated wholly or partly by racial hostility, or can show the existence of racial hostility (provided here by the mobile phone recorded evidence) at the time of the offence, the maximum sentence can be significantly increased by the court compared to an offence that is not racially motivated.

There are a number of responses the youth worker can take, one of which is the reporting of the incident to the police. One of the challenges facing the worker might be how to use the opportunity to address racism directly with the young people involved and among a wider group of young people with whom they are working and sending a clear message to other young people about intolerance of unacceptable, racist behaviour. There will be many opportunities throughout your professional work to address discrimination and you might well have clear ideas about how you can incorporate this into your practice on an ongoing basis rather than simply waiting for incidents such as this to arise.

Can you think of ways you might address homophobic or sexist language among young people? What about abusive terms for people with disabilities which are often used thoughtlessly by young people? The Special Educational Needs and Disability Act 2001 places duties on youth workers to make reasonable adjustments to ensure young people with disabilities are not treated less favourably. Are you confident that your professional practice meets the standards expected and articulated in the National Occupational Standards?

You might want to have a look at Table 1.1 which sets out the standards framework. You will notice that the essential knowledge and skills requirements are listed as:

- understanding of the impact of the broader social environment on young people's learning and development and of your own role and responsibilities as a professional worker;

- understanding of legislation, policy and practice which underpins a young person's human rights and basic entitlement;

- understanding the perspectives and motivations of others and the impact of your own actions and behaviours;

- understanding of the political environment and ethical framework within which youth work takes place;

- understanding of the learning needs of others and the leadership qualities needed to create a sense of common purpose.

The second-level functions are those that describe the tasks and role you will need to undertake to meet each broad category of competencies. The knowledge and skills you will need to undertake these tasks are important. While they are about your level of understanding and your ability to work effectively, they do not mention the values that are essential to your ability to execute this key role with integrity.

Values into action

One of the challenges facing the professional worker is that discriminatory language and behaviour are by-products of deeply held beliefs and values. In order to effectively tackle particular types of oppressive behaviour there is a requirement to undertake an examination of our own values and beliefs. During your studies, you will have many opportunities to explore your beliefs and motivations. You might find that some of these are open to challenge and this is part of the learning you can expect if you are to be a competent practitioner.

For example, a recent survey into domestic violence showed that almost a fifth of young people questioned believed that a man had a right to hit his partner if she dressed in a way that he believed to be provocative. If young people are to be challenged about beliefs that have the potential to harm others, the professional worker must be prepared to do likewise.

ACTIVITY *8.3*

Our values are influenced by our background and our upbringing. They can be shaped by our faith, our life experiences or our sense of self-worth.

Make a list of the things you value most, then sort them into ascending order and choose the six that mean most to you.

When you have done this, exclude those that are about love, family or friendship. What values remain? Do you see how these values you hold help to define your approach to your work with young people?

Did you include openness, honesty and integrity?

What about justice, fairness and equality?

Your values are likely to be the main factors influencing your choice of career as well as your progression within it. Your values have a direct influence on your preferred methods of working as well as on your behaviour. The occupational standards for youth work (Lifelong Learning UK) describe this as an ability to *recognise your own ethical, moral and cultural values and beliefs, and understand how this influences the way in which you work with young people* (NOS 1.3.1).

Your stated commitment to equality, diversity and fairness is not enough; you must be able to demonstrate that you:

- model behaviour that demonstrates a commitment to inclusion, equality of opportunity and the valuing of diversity;
- challenge constructively the status quo and seek better alternatives;
- treat others with respect and act to uphold their rights;
- demonstrate a clear understanding of different groups and their needs;
- make time available to support others;
- demonstrate integrity, fairness and consistency in decision making;
- communicate clearly, concisely and accurately;
- are vigilant for potential breaches of requirements;
- make appropriate information available promptly to those who need it and have a right to it.

Summary of key learning points

In Chapter 2 we looked at the impact of European law on UK policy and legislation. Prior to the implementation of a raft of legislation to combat discriminatory practice against women and on the grounds of race, and well before the implementation of the HRA, we relied on the European Courts as the final arbiter of justice when allegations of discrimination arose. However, you will remember from the discussion of the Article 14 rights within the ECHR that this provision did not stand alone. A person could only rely on it if one or more of the other provisions had been breached. This meant that they had to show that their freedom to express themselves or to associate with others had been restricted, and that the grounds for doing so were discriminatory.

The process was excessively long although there were some notable decisions against the UK, which set in place some of the changes we have made in the last 30 years to tackle oppressive practice. Although outside the scope of this book, you can read about some of them in any textbook on cases and materials of civil liberties and human rights. Many of the changes in UK law are still the subject of test cases on interpretation and sometimes the courts are expected to make judgments about whether or not we have achieved the right balance between individual situations and the wider social need in a democratic society.

Some of the challenges ahead

Inevitably there are new challenges for youth work in the twenty-first century. The increase in serious wounding and fatalities among young people in some of our cities is a cause for concern, particularly when in a survey conducted in 2005 (Marshall *et al.*) a significant number of young men reportedly admitted to carrying weapons for protection.

Some communities are disproportionately affected by what seems to be a culture of knife and gun crime and there is an expectation within the Youth Crime Action Plan that youth workers will work alongside the police to address gang membership among young people. In a televised interview with the Prime Minister, a 13-year-old boy from Peckham in South London asked Gordon Brown how he could be protected from being attacked. In the light of all these incidents there is some fear that hard-won freedoms are being eroded as ever-tighter prohibition on young people's freedom of movement and association prevails.

There is an increase in the number of young people presenting at an early age with mental health problems, which presents some scope for professional workers to address early pre-dictive factors rather than relying solely on diversion, treatment and incarceration. Despite some improvement in outcomes for young people leaving care, a disproportionate number of young people who have been in public care become involved in offending, become homeless or live in unsatisfactory accommodation and have few support net-works. It is estimated that a significant number of homeless young people find themselves in this situation as a consequence of being temporarily housed in unsuitable bed and breakfast accommodation because of a lack of supported housing. There is a significant number of adults with mental health problems who were formerly looked after by the local authority and too many young people presenting for treatment as a result of dependence on substances.

Concerns about the number of young people within some communities being taken out of the country for the purposes of marriage has led to changes in legislation through the Forced Marriage (Civil Protection) Act 2007. Under the legislation, workers who have con-cerns about a young person at risk can, with the leave of the court, apply for an order to protect the young person (Section 3.3 of schedule 1, part 1).

A way forward

However, despite the challenges, there are some outstanding examples of good practice in integrated youth provision across the country. You can read some of the case studies on the National Youth Association website or contained within OFSTED inspection reports. There are examples of young people using new media to find a voice in spite of some of the obstacles they face; of becoming involved in dramatic arts, music and sport; of taking part in campaigns and becoming involved in youth councils. There is as much for the professional worker to be proud of as there is to do.

Hopefully you feel a little better equipped with a basic knowledge of the law as it impacts on young people's human rights and you are sufficiently interested to share some of these ideas with young people so that they are better informed and able to access further information as they need it. This will not only help you to be a more effective advocate for the young people with whom you work but, more importantly, will empower them to advocate on their own behalf and have some confidence in their own ability to contribute to a fair and just society.

C H A P T E R   R E V I E W

- Professional youth work status is acquired through a higher educational study route leading to one of the following nationally recognised qualifications:

  - a Diploma in Higher Education (Dip HE);

  - a BA (Hons) degree;

  - a postgraduate certificate and (MA) Masters degree.

- From September 2010 there is a requirement that all new youth work qualifications must be at degree level or higher. As the changes are not retrospective, youth work qualifications acquired before this date will be valid.

- Youth workers have particular obligations to work in ways that promote inclusion and anti-oppressive practice, both among colleagues and with young people, so will need a good understanding of how the law operates and how the profession is regulated.

- Changes to the children and young people's workforce have come about as a direct consequence of failures in leadership and accountability and there is an expectation that youth workers, in common with all those working with young people, will set and maintain high standards.

- Changes in the law over the last ten years have made it easier to challenge discriminatory practice directly although there is recognition that we still have some way to go.

FURTHER READING

Bailey, SH, Harris, DJ and Jones, BL (2005) *Civil liberties cases and materials*, 4th edn. London: Butterworths.

Beebee, S and Cane, T (2002) *Good practice guide for youth workers and youth services – Special Educational Needs and Disability Act 2001.* Leicester: National Youth Agency.

Fenwick, H (2002) *Civil liberties and human rights*, 3rd edn. London: Cavendish.

Marshall, B, Webb, B and Tilley, N (2005) *Rationalisation of current research on guns, gangs and other weapons: Phase 1.* London: UCL.

WEBSITES

The National Youth Agency (NYA) Guide to Youth Work and Youth Services. **www.nya.org.uk/information/108737/nyaguidetoyouthworkandyouthservices/**

Lifelong Learning UK (2008) *National Occupational Standards.* **www.lluk.org/national-occupational-standards.htm**

REFERENCES

Offences Against the Person Act 1861. London: HMSO.

Sex Discrimination Act 1975. London: HMSO.

Race Relations Act 1976. London: HMSO.

Disability Discrimination Act 1995. London: HMSO.

Crime and Disorder Act 1998. London: The Stationery Office.

Race Relations (Amendment) Act 2000. London: The Stationery Office.

Sexual Offences (Amendment) Act 2000. London: The Stationery Office.

Special Educational Needs and Disability Act 2001. London: The Stationery Office.

Disability Discrimination Act 2005. London: The Stationery Office.

Youth matters Green Paper 2005. London: The Stationery Office.

Forced Marriage (Civil Protection) Act 2007. London: The Stationery Office.

Youth crime action plan 2008. London: The Stationery Office

Council of Europe (2002) *Convention for the protection of human rights and fundamental freedoms.* Strasbourg: Council of Europe.

Department for Education and Skills (2006) *Youth matters: next steps.* London: DFES.

Department for Education and Skills (2007) *Aiming high for young people: ten year strategy for positive activities.* London: DfES.

Laming, Lord (2003) *The Victoria Climbié inquiry: report of an inquiry by Lord Laming.* London: Department of Health.

Laming, Lord (2009) *The protection of children in England: a progress report.* London: The Stationery Office.

Lifelong Learning UK (2008) *National occupational standards for youth work.* London: Lifelong Learning UK.

Macpherson, W (1999) *The Stephen Lawrence Inquiry.* CMD 4262–I. London: The Stationery Office.

National Youth Agency (2000) *Ethical Conduct in Youth Work.* Leicester: National Youth Agency – **www.nya.org.uk**

Appendix 1

Summary of the purpose of the Human Rights Act 1998

An Act to give further effect to rights and freedoms guaranteed under the European Convention on Human Rights

Section 2 of the Act specifies how to interpret the European Convention on Human Rights (ECHR)

Section 2 Interpretation of Convention rights

(1) A court or tribunal determining a question which has arisen in connection with a Convention right must take into account any—

   (a) judgment, decision, declaration or advisory opinion of the European Court of Human Rights;

   (b) opinion of the Commission given in a report adopted under Article 31 of the Convention;

   (c) decision of the Commission in connection with Article 26 or 27(2) of the Convention; or

   (d) decision of the Committee of Ministers taken under Article 46 of the Convention, whenever made or given, so far as, in the opinion of the court or tribunal, it is relevant to the proceedings in which that question has arisen.

Section 3 Interpretation of legislation

(1) So far as it is possible to do so, primary legislation and subordinate legislation must be read and given effect in a way which is compatible with the Convention rights.

(2) This section:

   (a) applies to primary legislation and subordinate legislation whenever enacted;

   (b) does not affect the validity, continuing operation or enforcement of any incompatible primary legislation; and

(c) does not affect the validity, continuing operation or enforcement of any incompatible subordinate legislation if (disregarding any possibility of revocation) primary legislation prevents removal of the incompatibility.

Section 4 Declaration of incompatibility

(1) Subsection (2) applies in any proceedings in which a court determines whether a provision of primary legislation is compatible with a Convention right.

(2) If the court is satisfied that the provision is incompatible with a Convention right, it may make a declaration of that incompatibility.

Section 6 specifies the obligation of public authorities to act in a way that is compatible with the Convention and defines public authorities as:

(3) In this section 'public authority' includes—

(a) a court or tribunal; and

(b) any person certain of whose functions are functions of a public nature,

but does not include either House of Parliament or a person exercising functions in connection with proceedings in parliament.

Appendix 2

Convention for the Protection of Human Rights and Fundamental Freedoms, as amended by Protocol No. 11

The governments signatory hereto, being members of the Council of Europe,

Considering the Universal Declaration of Human Rights proclaimed by the General Assembly of the United Nations on 10th December 1948;

Considering that this Declaration aims at securing the universal and effective recognition and observance of the Rights therein declared;

Considering that the aim of the Council of Europe is the achievement of greater unity between its members and that one of the methods by which that aim is to be pursued is the maintenance and further realisation of human rights and fundamental freedoms;

Reaffirming their profound belief in those fundamental freedoms which are the foundation of justice and peace in the world and are best maintained on the one hand by an effective political democracy and on the other by a common understanding and observance of the human rights upon which they depend;

Being resolved, as the governments of European countries which are like-minded and have a common heritage of political traditions, ideals, freedom and the rule of law, to take the first steps for the collective enforcement of certain of the rights stated in the Universal Declaration,

Have agreed as follows:

Article 1 – Obligation to respect human rights

The High Contracting Parties shall secure to everyone within their jurisdiction the rights and freedoms defined in Section I of this Convention.

Section I – Rights and freedoms

Article 2 – Right to life

1 Everyone's right to life shall be protected by law. No one shall be deprived of his life intentionally save in the execution of a sentence of a court following his conviction of a crime for which this penalty is provided by law.

2 Deprivation of life shall not be regarded as inflicted in contravention of this Article when it results from the use of force which is no more than absolutely necessary:

   a in defence of any person from unlawful violence;

   b in order to effect a lawful arrest or to prevent the escape of a person lawfully detained;

   c in action lawfully taken for the purpose of quelling a riot or insurrection.

Article 3 – Prohibition of torture

No one shall be subjected to torture or to inhuman or degrading treatment or punishment.

Article 4 – Prohibition of slavery and forced labour

1 No one shall be held in slavery or servitude.

2 No one shall be required to perform forced or compulsory labour.

3 For the purpose of this Article the term 'forced or compulsory labour' shall not include:

   a any work required to be done in the ordinary course of detention imposed according to the provisions of Article 5 of this Convention or during conditional release from such detention;

   b any service of a military character or, in case of conscientious objectors in countries where they are recognised, service exacted instead of compulsory military service;

   c any service exacted in case of an emergency or calamity threatening the life or well-being of the community;

   d any work or service which forms part of normal civic obligations.

Article 5 – Right to liberty and security

1 Everyone has the right to liberty and security of person. No one shall be deprived of his liberty save in the following cases and in accordance with a procedure prescribed by law:

   a the lawful detention of a person after conviction by a competent court;

   b the lawful arrest or detention of a person for non-compliance with the lawful order of a court or in order to secure the fulfilment of any obligation prescribed by law;

c the lawful arrest or detention of a person effected for the purpose of bringing him before the competent legal authority on reasonable suspicion of having committed an offence or when it is reasonably considered necessary to prevent his committing an offence or fleeing after having done so;

d the detention of a minor by lawful order for the purpose of educational supervision or his lawful detention for the purpose of bringing him before the competent legal authority;

e the lawful detention of persons for the prevention of the spreading of infectious diseases, of persons of unsound mind, alcoholics or drug addicts or vagrants;

f the lawful arrest or detention of a person to prevent his effecting an unauthorised entry into the country or of a person against whom action is being taken with a view to deportation or extradition.

2 Everyone who is arrested shall be informed promptly, in a language which he understands, of the reasons for his arrest and of any charge against him.

3 Everyone arrested or detained in accordance with the provisions of paragraph 1.c of this Article shall be brought promptly before a judge or other officer authorised by law to exercise judicial power and shall be entitled to trial within a reasonable time or to release pending trial. Release may be conditioned by guarantees to appear for trial.

4 Everyone who is deprived of his liberty by arrest or detention shall be entitled to take proceedings by which the lawfulness of his detention shall be decided speedily by a court and his release ordered if the detention is not lawful.

5 Everyone who has been the victim of arrest or detention in contravention of the provisions of this Article shall have an enforceable right to compensation.

Article 6 – Right to a fair trial

1 In the determination of his civil rights and obligations or of any criminal charge against him, everyone is entitled to a fair and public hearing within a reasonable time by an independent and impartial tribunal established by law. Judgment shall be pronounced publicly but the press and public may be excluded from all or part of the trial in the interests of morals, public order or national security in a democratic society, where the interests of juveniles or the protection of the private life of the parties so require, or to the extent strictly necessary in the opinion of the court in special circumstances where publicity would prejudice the interests of justice.

2 Everyone charged with a criminal offence shall be presumed innocent until proved guilty according to law.

3 Everyone charged with a criminal offence has the following minimum rights:

a to be informed promptly, in a language which he understands and in detail, of the nature and cause of the accusation against him;

b to have adequate time and facilities for the preparation of his defence;

c to defend himself in person or through legal assistance of his own choosing or, if he has not sufficient means to pay for legal assistance, to be given it free when the interests of justice so require;

d to examine or have examined witnesses against him and to obtain the attendance and examination of witnesses on his behalf under the same conditions as witnesses against him;

e to have the free assistance of an interpreter if he cannot understand or speak the language used in court.

Article 7 – No punishment without law

1 No one shall be held guilty of any criminal offence on account of any act or omission which did not constitute a criminal offence under national or international law at the time when it was committed. Nor shall a heavier penalty be imposed than the one that was applicable at the time the criminal offence was committed.

2 This Article shall not prejudice the trial and punishment of any person for any act or omission which, at the time when it was committed, was criminal according to the general principles of law recognised by civilised nations.

Article 8 – Right to respect for private and family life

1 Everyone has the right to respect for his private and family life, his home and his correspondence.

2 There shall be no interference by a public authority with the exercise of this right except such as is in accordance with the law and is necessary in a democratic society in the interests of national security, public safety or the economic wellbeing of the country, for the prevention of disorder or crime, for the protection of health or morals, or for the protection of the rights and freedoms of others.

Article 9 – Freedom of thought, conscience and religion

1 Everyone has the right to freedom of thought, conscience and religion; this right includes freedom to change his religion or belief and freedom, either alone or in community with others and in public or private, to manifest his religion or belief, in worship, teaching, practice and observance.

2 Freedom to manifest one's religion or beliefs shall be subject only to such limitations as are prescribed by law and are necessary in a democratic society in the interests of public safety, for the protection of public order, health or morals, or for the protection of the rights and freedoms of others.

Article 10 – Freedom of expression

1 Everyone has the right to freedom of expression. This right shall include freedom to hold opinions and to receive and impart information and ideas without interference by public authority and regardless of frontiers. This Article shall not prevent States from requiring the licensing of broadcasting, television or cinema enterprises.

2 The exercise of these freedoms, since it carries with it duties and responsibilities, may be subject to such formalities, conditions, restrictions or penalties as are prescribed by law and are necessary in a democratic society, in the interests of national security, territorial integrity or public safety, for the prevention of disorder or crime, for the protection of health or morals, for the protection of the reputation or rights of others, for preventing the disclosure of information received in confidence, or for maintaining the authority and impartiality of the judiciary.

Article 11 – Freedom of assembly and association

1 Everyone has the right to freedom of peaceful assembly and to freedom of association with others, including the right to form and to join trade unions for the protection of his interests.

2 No restrictions shall be placed on the exercise of these rights other than such as are prescribed by law and are necessary in a democratic society in the interests of national security or public safety, for the prevention of disorder or crime, for the protection of health or morals or for the protection of the rights and freedoms of others. This Article shall not prevent the imposition of lawful restrictions on the exercise of these rights by members of the armed forces, of the police or of the administration of the State.

Article 12 – Right to marry

Men and women of marriageable age have the right to marry and to found a family, according to the national laws governing the exercise of this right.

Article 13 – Right to an effective remedy

Everyone whose rights and freedoms as set forth in this Convention are violated shall have an effective remedy before a national authority notwithstanding that the violation has been committed by persons acting in an official capacity.

Article 14 – Prohibition of discrimination

The enjoyment of the rights and freedoms set forth in this Convention shall be secured without discrimination on any ground such as sex, race, colour, language, religion, political or other opinion, national or social origin, association with a national minority, property, birth or other status.

Article 15 – Derogation in time of emergency

1 In time of war or other public emergency threatening the life of the nation any High Contracting Party may take measures derogating from its obligations under this Convention to the extent strictly required by the exigencies of the situation, provided that such measures are not inconsistent with its other obligations under international law.

2 No derogation from Article 2, except in respect of deaths resulting from lawful acts of war, or from Articles 3, 4 (paragraph 1) and 7 shall be made under this provision.

3 Any High Contracting Party availing itself of this right of derogation shall keep the Secretary General of the Council of Europe fully informed of the measures which it has taken and the reasons therefor. It shall also inform the Secretary General of the Council of Europe when such measures have ceased to operate and the provisions of the Convention are again being fully executed.

Article 16 – Restrictions on political activity of aliens

Nothing in Articles 10, 11 and 14 shall be regarded as preventing the High Contracting Parties from imposing restrictions on the political activity of aliens.

Article 17 – Prohibition of abuse of rights

Nothing in this Convention may be interpreted as implying for any State, group or person any right to engage in any activity or perform any act aimed at the destruction of any of the rights and freedoms set forth herein or at their limitation to a greater extent than is provided for in the Convention.

Article 18 – Limitation on use of restrictions on rights

The restrictions permitted under this Convention to the said rights and freedoms shall not be applied for any purpose other than those for which they have been prescribed.

Section II – European Court of Human Rights

Article 19 – Establishment of the Court

To ensure the observance of the engagements undertaken by the High Contracting Parties in the Convention and the Protocols thereto, there shall be set up a European Court of Human Rights, hereinafter referred to as 'the Court'. It shall function on a permanent basis.

Article 20 – Number of judges

The Court shall consist of a number of judges equal to that of the High Contracting Parties.

Article 21 – Criteria for office

1 The judges shall be of high moral character and must either possess the qualifications required for appointment to high judicial office or be jurisconsults of recognised competence.

2 The judges shall sit on the Court in their individual capacity.

3 During their term of office the judges shall not engage in any activity which is incompatible with their independence, impartiality or with the demands of a full-time office; all questions arising from the application of this paragraph shall be decided by the Court.

Appendix 3
Table of cases

A v. *UK* (human rights punishment of child) (1988) 27 EHRR 611

A (children) (conjoined twins: surgical separation), RE [2000] 1 FCR 193, 53 BMLR 66

B (children) (FC). [2008] UKHL 35.

Costello-Roberts v. *UK* (1993) 19 EHRR 112 [1994] 1 FCR65

Gillick v. *West Norfolk Health Authority* [1986] AC 112, [1985] All ER 533

Goodwin v. *UK,* (Application no. 28957/95) Judgment of 11/07/2002

Leander v. *Sweden* (1987) 9 EHRR 433

Mandla v. *Lee* [1983] 2 AC 548, [1983] 1 All ER 1062, [1983] 2 WLR 620, [1983] IC R 385, [1983] HL

Neilsen v. *Denmark* (1988) 11 EHRR 175

Phelps v. *London Borough of Hillingdon* [2001] 2AC 619

Pretty v. *United Kingdom* (Application no.2346/02). Judgment of 29/04/2002

PW, R (on the application of) v. *Commissioner of Police for the Metropolis & Anor* [2006] EWCA Civ 458 (11 May 2006)

R v. *Kirklees MBC ex p C* [1997] 2 FLR 180

R v. *Brown* [1993] 2 All ER 75, (HL)

Sue Axon v. *The Secretary Of State for Health* (The Family Planning Association: intervening) [2006] EWCA 37 (Admin)

R [1992] Fam 11, (1992) 7 BMLR 147

R (A Minor) (Wardship; Medical Treatment) [1991] 4 All E.R. 177, [1922] Fam 11, [1991] 3 W.L.R. 592

Singh v. *Aberdare Girls' High School and Rhondda Cynon Taf Unitary Authority* (2008) Case No: CO/11435/2007 QBD

T v. *UK; V* v. *UK* (2000) 30 EHRR 121

W (A Minor) (Medical Treatment: Court's Jurisdiction [1993] 1FLR 1)

Z and TP and KM (T.P. and K.M.) v. *UK,* (Application no. 28945/95) 10 May 2001: (2002) 34 EHRR 3

Index